ENDORSEMENTS

At last a book focusing on a much-needed topic for women! Redemption is the core of our faith. This truly engaging book will not only enlighten but inspire readers!

—Beverly Lewis
New York Times bestselling author of Amish fiction

I love Kerry Clarensau's heart for women! With bold yet tender words, she comes alongside as a friend, pointing us to a Father who loves us beyond our worst mistakes and a Savior who redeems, restores, and makes everything new.

—Joanna Weaver
Bestselling author of *Having a Mary Heart in a Martha World*

When Kerry first shared with me the thoughts the Lord had given her for *Redeemed!*, I felt a sense of awe and knew for sure that this book was going to be a life-changer for many. Having read it, the awe has turned to praise—to the Lord for giving her the outline and inspiration and to Kerry for her ability to take those divine thoughts and wield them into a masterpiece that will impact the lives of women worldwide.

—JoAnn Butrin, PhD
Director of International Ministries, Assemblies of God

Certain words with faith associations sometimes lose their punch and poignancy through the years because they're either overused, misused, or under-appreciated. *Redeemed* is a word I've sung, spoken, and heard countless times through my decades of following Jesus. After reading *Redeemed! Embracing a Transformed Life,* that word has taken on a new vibrancy that feels an awful lot like hope . . . hope that redemption doesn't end with a decision to trust Christ—it really just *begins* there and it touches every part of life!

It takes a person like Kerry, with a heart like hers, to mine the treasures out of a word like *redeemed*—because it's more than a word; it's a life-changing concept. Read this powerful book and get ready to be transformed!

—Jodi Detrick
Chairperson for the Network for Women in Ministry, columnist for *The Seattle Times,* author of *The Jesus-Hearted Woman,* speaker, and life-coach

If you are ready for a truly new adventure with God, this book will take you on a life-changing journey! We all have the tendency to ignore the parts of ourselves that Jesus wants to renew; we accept things as status quo. Kerry provides a blueprint for an extreme makeover—"inside" edition—unlocking the keys to an extravagantly transformed life! This work of art is essential for every twenty-first century woman who desires to experience a revitalized life of freedom and purpose.

—Dr. Ava Oleson
Doctor of Ministry Program Coordinator, Adjunct Professor, Assemblies of God Theological Seminary

There is no more marvelous subject than the glorious redemption offered to us by our Savior. Kerry Clarensau has done a masterful job of showing how to experience that wonderful miracle in every area of a woman's life. This study will be life changing for all those who open this book and engage its truth. Study it and share it with a friend!

—Dr. George O. Wood
General Superintendent of the Assemblies of God

When the power of God washes over our lives, a wonderful redemption begins to rise from the ash heap of brokenness and failure. And that gift is available to all who seek it. Kerry Clarensau offers the help you need to experience that redemption in your life and to discover freedom to be the disciple you were designed to be.

—L. Alton Garrison
Assistant General Superintendent of the Assemblies of God

Redeemed!

EMBRACING A TRANSFORMED LIFE

BY KERRY CLARENSAU

FOREWORD BY CAROL KENT

MY HEALTHY CHURCH
MyHealthyChurch.com

Published by My Healthy Church
1445 North Boonville Avenue
Springfield, Missouri 65802

Published in association with The Quadrivium Group—Orlando, Florida
info@TheQuadriviumGroup.com.
Typesetting by Prodigy Pixel, www.prodigypixel.com
Cover design by Harp Creative, LLC., www.harpcreative.com

ISBN: 978-1-62423-027-1
First printing 2012
Printed in the United States of America

---

*This book is dedicated to the next generations of women in my family—
my daughter-in-law, Katie; my sweet grandbaby, Molly Jayne;
and my nieces, Bethany, Korie, Chelsea, and Chloe.
I loved you before you were born!
May God's grace continue to transform you into
the women you were designed to be!*

CONTENTS

Foreword   1

Introduction   5

CHAPTER 1   Embracing Our Redeemer   17

CHAPTER 2   Redeeming Our Past   55

CHAPTER 3   Redeeming Our Perspective   89

CHAPTER 4   Redeeming Our Sexuality   127

CHAPTER 5   Redeeming Relationships   169

CHAPTER 6   Redeeming the Time   211

APPENDIX A   The "I Am" Passages of Jesus   253

APPENDIX B   Biblical Guidelines for
             Healthy Relationships   259

FOREWORD

by Carol Kent

The weekend women's conference was filled with Divine surprises, and my heart was singing with all God had done. Many women had come to faith in Christ, and the altar was filled after every session with women who were laying their prayer needs before the Lord. After saying my goodbyes to the conference team, I had a luncheon appointment with a woman from the church who was in charge of an expanding jail ministry to female inmates. I liked her immediately.

After ordering our meals, I said, "Julie, how did you first get interested in ministering to inmates?" She smiled and paused, as if evaluating how much of her journey to share.

Tearing up, she said, "I was in an intensely abusive marriage, and when my children were young, my husband was not willing to make the funds I needed for their basic food and clothing available. At the time, I was working in my church office, and my part-time hours fluctuated greatly from week to week. The treasurer would drop off a signed blank check and let me fill in my own salary. School was starting in one week, and I rationalized that I could add a little extra to my check to cover the needed funds. The following week, I did the same thing, and before long, I was adding enough to my salary that it covered my wants, and not just my needs. Years passed, and I continued to embezzle funds from my church, which eventually totaled in the thousands of dollars."

Julie continued. "Eventually, I could no longer live with myself. My children were almost grown, and I knew I had to make things right, even though it might mean going to prison. One afternoon, I went to my pastor and shared honestly about the funds I had stolen from the church. He was more compassionate than I deserved, but a matter of this importance had to go before the church board."

By this time Julie was choking back tears, and then she said, "These remarkable Christian people did the unexpected. Instead of having me arrested, they forgave me and worked out a plan for restitution that I am still paying back to this day. I experienced redemption in the fullest sense of the word— freedom from the consequences of my sin, an opportunity to change for the better, restoration, release from guilt, and the opportunity to pay back my debt and live as a transformed woman. I received the opposite of what I deserved—and that's why I'm investing my life in ministering to incarcerated women."

Kerry Clarensau has written a book that gives each of us a tool for learning how to embrace a transformed life. Many of us think we understand what it's like to be redeemed from the consequences of our wrong choices—but this book helps us to learn the secrets of applying God's Word to our lives in a way that leads to overcoming past mistakes, understanding who we are in Christ, becoming women of worth, engaging in meaningful relationships, and making the most of the time God has given us.

My favorite parts of the book are the clear, biblical teachings, the personal illustrations, the practical strategies for personal and spiritual growth, and the group discussion questions that produce opportunities for women to be honest with each other in small groups that will foster deepening friendships. This book is powerful for personal study, but it is even more enriching when you discuss each point with a friend, or a small group of friends. Thanks, Kerry, for giving us a book that will help us to go deeper with God and with each other! I highly recommend *Redeemed! Embracing a Transformed Life!*

—**Carol Kent,** Speaker and Author
Becoming a Woman of Influence (Navpress)
www.CarolKent.org

INTRODUCTION

Put your hope in the LORD, for with the LORD is
unfailing love and with him is full redemption.
PSALM 130:7

T he other day I pulled my favorite black cardigan out of the
closet and discovered a large bleach stain on the front of
it. I should know better than to clean my house wearing dress
clothes! But the sweater is ruined—unless bleach-dyed sweaters
become fashionable someday. I'm sure you know the feeling.
We've all had that favorite piece of clothing get damaged.

Sadly, clothes aren't the only things in life that can seem
ruined. Mistakes create shame, careless words wound the heart,
and disappointments steal hope. Even if we don't feel damaged,
our life may not be all we hoped it would be. But while there
isn't hope for my sweater, there is hope for us! And that's what
this book is all about.

Because of the impact of sin, every one of us needs
redemption. In fact, every harmful thing in our life is a direct
result of sin. We make choices to sin, those around us choose to
sin, and all of those choices create pain. Sin not only harms us,
it separates us from one another and causes conflict and power
struggles. Sin steals the good things in life, leaving a wake of
strife in its path.

We were created by God to know Him and enjoy life
with Him. But sin not only separates us from one another, it
separates us from God. He is perfect, and we know we can never

measure up to His standards on our own. Our sin causes shame, makes us want to hide, and creates a barrier between us and God. In His great mercy, God loved us so much that He made a way for us to receive forgiveness and enjoy a relationship with Him through His Son, Jesus. "For God so loved the world that he gave his one and only Son, that whoever believes in him shall not perish but have eternal life. For God did not send his Son into the world to condemn the world, but to save the world through him" (John 3:16–17).

Jesus did some amazing things while He was here on earth. First of all, being fully human, He showed us what it's like for us to live in a close relationship with our heavenly Father. Secondly, being fully God, He showed us exactly what God is like. If we ever want to know what God thinks, what He would say, or how He would treat someone, we simply have to read the account of Jesus' life in the Gospels.

Since Jesus is the only one to live a completely sinless life, He is the only one capable of paying for our sins. Jesus, in perfect love, willingly paid the price with His death on the cross. Then through His resurrection, He became our Redeemer—declaring His victory over death and hell!

In him we have *redemption* through his blood, the forgiveness of sins, in accordance with the riches of God's grace that he lavished on us.
(EPH. 1:7–8, EMPHASIS MINE)

When we accept Jesus as our Savior and ask Him to forgive us, God completely removes our sins and never holds them against us again. When He looks at us, He no longer sees our sins. He sees the righteousness of Christ. (What an *amazing* thing!) Along with forgiveness comes the promise of spending eternity in heaven with our Creator. And there is even more! Between our salvation and heaven, He wants us to experience transformation. He longs to remove the effect sin has had in our lives!

He wants us to embrace a relationship with Him that will completely transform every part of our lives. His grace can redeem the scars of our past, our perspective, and our sexuality. He longs to lead us to life-giving relationships with one another. And He can help us to make the absolute most of our time here on earth! "For it is by grace you have been saved, through faith—and this is not from yourselves, it is the gift of God— not by works, so that no one can boast. For we are God's handiwork created in Christ Jesus to do good works, which God prepared in advance for us to do" (Eph. 2:8–10, NIV).

A PICTURE OF REDEMPTION

Have you ever been struck by a woman's *countenance?* You find her very presence appealing? I'm not talking about external beauty or a sense of style but something about a woman that makes you want to know her. That's how I felt when I met Peggy Musgrove twenty-five years ago.

The first time I talked to her was on a busy Oklahoma City sidewalk. My husband, Mike, and I were there with our three-year-old son, Tyler, for a conference. We saw the Musgroves one afternoon, and they stopped to greet us. It's funny what you remember and what you don't. I can't tell you what we talked about, but I distinctly remember how Tyler's little hand felt in mine and the impact Peggy made on me.

She was humble, yet confident. (I know . . . that seems like a contradiction, right?) She was sincere—there was nothing showy or pretentious about her. She was kind and attentive, not distracted by the crowd of people around us. I felt like she really saw us; she even acknowledged Tyler and spoke to him with respect, helping him to feel included in the conversation. Her words were positive and encouraging. Immediately, she won my heart, and I hoped I would get to know her better.

Not long after that brief encounter in Oklahoma, I began working with Peggy in our home state of Kansas. Our work relationship spanned more than a decade, two states, and three different positions. As I got to know her better, I discovered that my first impressions were only partially accurate. Yes, she is all of those things I saw immediately, but she is so much more. She is a woman who has allowed God's grace to transform her *continually*. Those who know her well would agree with me—the more you get to know Peggy, the more you see to admire. (Isn't it sad how some people appear better from a distance than they do up close? Not Peggy!)

Being an up-close observer of Peggy's life, I saw her treat everyone with respect. She always managed conflict with grace and integrity. She didn't speak negatively about people or begrudge difficult situations. Her joy and peace were evident by-products of a deep awareness of God's presence. Peggy's words resounded with wisdom and her knowledge of God's Word. She firmly believed that God led her steps, and He would faithfully provide what was needed for every challenge along the way. Her love for people was always apparent—she consistently wanted what was best for everyone in her life.

A lot has changed since I first met Peggy. I'm no longer a young mom with a toddler. I'm now a "grammy" of a toddler. And Peggy is in her eighties—more humble and gracious than ever before, but her confidence in God today is absolutely inspiring. Her precious husband of sixty-two years is very ill. She spends her days (and nights) lovingly caring for him—confident she is doing exactly what God wants her to do. Time and difficulties haven't diminished her spirit. In fact, her countenance is more Christ-like than ever before.

So how did Peggy become this woman? Was she simply born this way? No. Just like you and me, she was born with a sinful nature and into a family with its fair share of challenges. Her early life was significantly marked by the Depression, severe drought, and World War II. The Dust Bowl days devastated farms in western Kansas, so the family moved many times. Peggy lived in ten homes during her twelve years of schooling.

Growing up, Peggy was the only girl in a house full of boys— she had three brothers. In fact, she was the only female born into her dad's family in a fifty-year span. (We can only imagine the doting!) In spite of the special treatment she received from her grandparents and being loved by her family, she spent most of her childhood feeling like an outsider. Peggy's shy nature and always being the "new girl" at school hindered her from forming close relationships. While her mother was a strong Christian and a consistent role model for her, they only attended church intermittently.

At the age of nineteen, Peggy made a fresh commitment to follow Christ and decided to attend college. There she met Derald Musgrove, the fun, outgoing guy she would spend the next six decades loving and sharing life with.

Derald's love and support encouraged her to grow and mature into the woman she became. But Peggy would be the first to tell you that he isn't the most influential part of her life. She would want you to understand that who she is today is a direct result of the redeeming grace of Jesus Christ. My friend Peggy is a picture of a woman who received God's free gift of salvation and then, day-by-day, allowed Him to transform her character and lead her to the things He wanted her to do.

When reading Peggy's books and articles, you see how she has allowed God's truth to define her, guide her, and instruct her. He has lovingly used His Word and some challenging circumstances to sand away the misshapen places in her heart. Even today, at the age of eighty-two, she continually allows God's grace to wash over her. His mercy allows her to live with integrity, work with faithfulness, serve with humility, speak with kindness, act with wisdom, and love with fervency. Peggy walks through life with a noticeable peace and joy that isn't dependent upon ideal circumstances.

Through her years of faithfully walking with God, He led her to opportunities that were designed specifically for her. He allowed this shy, young woman from Western Kansas to lead ministries, author books, speak at conferences around the world, mentor many young women, raise two beautiful daughters, and love a man as well as any man has ever been loved.

While God planned many things for Peggy to accomplish, it's not her accomplishments you will admire the most. The appealing thing about Peggy is her redeemed, Christ-like character. I didn't realize it at the time, but what I saw on that hot Oklahoma sidewalk was genuine redemption. A redeemed life is really one of the most beautiful things on earth!

REDEMPTION DEFINED

Since we talk a lot about redemption, I thought you might like to read this definition of the word *redeem* from Merriam-Webster's dictionary:

1 *a* : to buy back : REPURCHASE *b* : to get or
win back
2 : to free from what distresses or harms: as *a* : to
free from captivity by payment of ransom
b : to extricate from or help to overcome
something detrimental *c* : to release from blame
or debt : CLEAR *d* : to free from the consequences
of sin
3 : to change for the better : REFORM
4 : REPAIR, RESTORE
5 *a* : to free from a lien by payment of an
amount secured thereby *b* (1) : to remove
the obligation of by payment <the United
States Treasury *redeems* savings bonds on
demand> (2) : to exchange for something of
value <*redeem* trading stamps> *c* : to make
good : FULFILL

6 *a* : to atone for : EXPIATE <*redeem* an error>
b (1) : to offset the bad effect of *(2)* : to make
worthwhile: RETRIEVE [1]

Reading those definitions helps us to understand what
Christ offers us in redemption:

- Freedom from the consequences of sin
- The opportunity to change for the better
- Restoration from the negative effects of sin
- Freedom from our debt of sin
- The possibility of living a life that is worthwhile

My friend Pam and I hosted a birthday celebration for
Peggy. We invited other women who had been significantly
impacted by her life. It was fun to hear the different things
Peggy had taught each of them. Becky (who flew in from Denver
for the party) shared how Peggy once told her, "Ninety percent
of success is just showing up." She knew Peggy was telling her
that when we are faithful to do what we can, we can trust God
to show up and do what only He can. (By the way, Peggy was
quick to tell us the quote wasn't original to her.)

Peggy has spent the last sixty-plus years faithfully showing
up and, just as He promised, God has molded her into a woman
after His own heart. Her character looks more like His every
day. He has allowed her to make the world around her a much
better place. She has known His peace, felt real joy, responded
faithfully in difficulty, and experienced the contentment of
doing His will.

God has a similar story He wants to write in your life!

With every thought about this book, I have fervently prayed for *you* to experience all God has planned for you. Salvation is a wonderful, free gift from our Redeemer. But the redemptive, transforming process requires our participation— one day at a time. When we faithfully do what we can, God does the rest. The apostle Peter encourages us with these words:

By his divine power, God has given us everything we need for living a godly life. We have received all of this by coming to know him, the one who called us to himself by means of his marvelous glory and excellence. And because of his glory and excellence, he has given us great and precious promises. These are the promises that enable you to share his divine nature and escape the world's corruption caused by human desires.

In view of all this, make every effort to respond to God's promises. Supplement your faith with a generous provision of moral excellence, and moral excellence with knowledge, and knowledge with self-control, and self-control with patient endurance, and patient endurance with godliness, and godliness with brotherly affection, and brotherly affection with love for everyone.

The more you grow like this, the more productive and useful you will be in your knowledge of our LORD Jesus Christ. But those who fail to develop in this way are shortsighted or blind, forgetting that they have been cleansed from their old sins.

So, dear brothers and sisters, work hard to prove that you really are among those God has called and chosen. Do these things, and you will never fall away. Then God will give you a grand entrance into the eternal Kingdom of our LORD and Savior Jesus Christ." (2 PET. 1:3–11, NLT)

I'm so thankful for God's redemption and excited for us to take this journey together. Let's embrace all He has in store for us!

SCAN THIS CODE
WITH YOUR
SMARTPHONE
TO WATCH
A VIDEO
INTRODUCTION
TO THIS CHAPTER.

CHAPTER ONE

Embracing Our Redeemer

This is what the LORD says—
your Redeemer, the Holy One of Israel:
"I am the LORD your God, who teaches you what is best for you,
who directs you in the way you should go.
If only you had paid attention to my commands,
your peace would have been like a river,
your well-being like the waves of the sea.

ISAIAH 48:17–18

I stood there thinking, *who was that crazy woman speaking to Tyler like that?* My fifteen-year-old son said something to set me off, and I mouthed a scathing response. *What on earth was I doing, engaging my son in this verbal battle? He's such a great kid! Why would I speak to him like that?* I didn't like what was happening to our relationship! Every day we were drifting farther apart. His words, his body language, and even his facial expressions seemed to infuriate me. *Why can't I control my own tongue?* Yes, he was responding like a teenager, but my responses were anything but helpful. My strong words and defensive demeanor simply added fuel to his already frustrated attitude.

I'm sure you get the picture. You may not have argued with an adolescent, but surely you've witnessed a similar discussion in an aisle at Wal-Mart or on a family television sitcom. It's embarrassing to admit that I have been that crazy mother— thankfully never at Wal-Mart, but definitely in the privacy of our own home.

One day, in the middle of a heated debate, I felt the Holy Spirit whisper into my heart, "Kerry, what are you doing? You don't have to respond to Tyler this way. I can help you to respond in the right way—with love, joy, peace, patience, kindness, goodness, faithfulness, gentleness and self-control." The Holy Spirit was kindly reminding me of Galatians 5:22–23, familiar verses I learned as a child. So that afternoon I decided to steal away from the busyness of my family and reread the passage one more time. Maybe I would find some insight in those verses to help me handle this exasperating situation.

Here is what I discovered. (On the left are the verses and to the right are my honest, extremely humbling responses.)

———— ⊗⊗⊗ ————

BIBLE VERSES	MY RESPONSE
[16] So I say, let the Holy Spirit guide your lives. Then you won't be doing what your sinful nature craves. [17] The sinful nature wants to do evil, which is just the opposite of what the Spirit wants. And the Spirit	(verses 16–18) *I'm definitely not allowing the Holy Spirit to guide my conversation with Tyler!*

gives us desires that are the opposite of what the sinful nature desires. These two forces are constantly fighting each other, so you are not free to carry out your good intentions. [13] But when you are directed by the Spirit you are not under obligation to the law of Moses.

[19] When you follow the desires of your sinful nature, the results are very clear: sexual immorality, impurity, lustful pleasures, [20] idolatry, sorcery, hostility, quarreling, jealousy, outbursts of anger, selfish ambition, dissension, division, [21] envy, drunkenness, wild parties, and other sins like these. Let me tell you again, as I have before, that anyone living that sort of life will not inherit the Kingdom of God.

[22] But the Holy Spirit produces this kind of fruit in our lives: love, joy, peace, patience, kindness, goodness, faithfulness, [23] gentleness, and self-control. There is no law against these things!

[24] Those who belong to Christ Jesus have nailed the passions and desires of their sinful nature to his cross and crucified them there. [25] Since we are living by the Spirit, let us follow the Spirit's leading in every part of our lives. [26] Let us not become conceited, or provoke one another, or be jealous of one another.

GALATIANS 5:16–26, NLT

My sinful nature takes control and I'm not giving the Holy Spirit a chance to respond.

(verses 19–21)
I'm experiencing several things on this list. Hostility? Well, yes, I've been rather hostile. Quarreling? Check. Outbursts of anger? Check. Okay, my sinful nature is in control, and it isn't pretty!

(verses 22–23)
The Holy Spirit produces some amazing qualities. This is exactly what I need, and what Tyler needs from me!

(verses 24–25)
I do want to allow the Holy Spirit to lead every part of my life— even my conversations with Tyler!

(verse 26)
I've got to stop provoking my son!

I was disappointed after that self-exam; I gave myself a D minus. But I asked God to forgive me and renewed my commitment to submit to the Holy Spirit's leading, even in the midst of intense moments with my fifteen-year-old son.

The next time my conversation with Tyler started to get heated, I could feel the "spirit of smack" come upon me (actually, that was just my sinful nature!). But instead of reacting in the way I felt, I took control of my tongue. Silently, I asked the Lord to help me respond to Tyler with His heart and words. What came out of my mouth was amazing—not at all what my initial response would have been. The words were soothing, like salve on wounds, not at all like the "gasoline" I had splashed on Tyler before. The Holy Spirit came through and helped me respond appropriately as I simply allowed Him to guide my words and the way in which I said them.

Tyler's reaction was completely different when he received patient, kind, self-controlled responses from his mother. His guard came down, and our conversations became healing, not toxic. I'm so thankful for the work of the Holy Spirit in my life, especially in this specific situation. I didn't get it right every time after that, but if I had consistently responded with my sinful nature, I would have driven Tyler away. Today we enjoy a fun, healthy relationship. Now that he is a father, I hope he learns this lesson sooner than I did. I really want him to know he can rely on the Holy Spirit to lead every part of his life—even the everyday, messy parts like emotional conversations with our children.

EVERY GOOD THING IN OUR LIVES IS FROM GOD, AND GRACE IS ONE OF THE BEST GIFTS OF ALL.

OUR REDEEMER

Let's take a moment to reread the verse for this chapter:

This is what the LORD says—your Redeemer, the Holy
One of Israel: "I am the LORD your God, who teaches
you what is best for you, who directs you in the way
you should go, If only you had paid attention to my
commands, your peace would have been like a river,
your well-being like the waves of the sea."
(ISA. 48:17–18)

I love the simple truth of this passage. Our Redeemer longs
to teach us what is best and to direct us in the way we should go.
Sometimes when we read passages like this one, we think the
direction the Lord offers is for major, life-changing decisions—
like who to marry or what job to take. But the relationship
He offers is much more encompassing. He actually wants to be
involved in every part of our lives, including our thoughts, our
words, our responses, even our attitudes!

God is the designer of life, and He knows exactly the best
way to live it. Did you catch the last part of that verse in Isaiah,
"If only you had paid attention to my commands, your peace
would have been like a river, your well-being like the waves of
the sea"? God wants to lavish our lives with His peace and lead
us to those things that are the absolute best for us.

The story I shared about my son Tyler is only one of many
personal examples I could share. There have been plenty of
moments when my sinful nature was in control and hindered
the Holy Spirit's leading. But the more seasoned I've become

(just a more positive way of saying "the older I get"), the more I've learned to embrace my Redeemer and allow Him to be the true leader of my life.

I've learned to trust God's love for me and depend fully on Him moment by moment. He doesn't always teach easy lessons or lead me to smooth paths, but I've consistently experienced the peace He promises in Isaiah 48. And the goodness He brings to my life when I submit to His leadership is worth every sacrifice along the way—like the good things He brought into my relationship with Tyler.

The decision to stop our sinful nature from responding is a moment-by-moment decision. Unfortunately, we will never be able to say, "I am *completely* Spirit-controlled!" It's a daily process of allowing the Holy Spirit to fill and lead our lives. So we shouldn't beat ourselves up for those moments when we allow our nature to take control—we can humbly repent and ask again for His help. The more we consciously depend upon the Holy Spirit to lead us, the more natural it becomes.

REDEMPTION

Many of us have heard children's songs that teach basic spiritual practices. One of those songs goes something like this, "Read your Bible, pray every day and you'll grow, grow, grow. And you'll grow, grow, grow . . . " (I remember bending down, almost sitting on my heels, and inching my way up as we sang, "and you'll grow, grow, grow.")

While those words are simple, their truth is profound. Our Redeemer has invited us to receive His grace and enter into a relationship with Him that will positively revolutionize our lives. But instead of simply considering how external activities like reading our Bible, praying, and going to church can have a positive impact on our lives, I want us to consider what it means to *embrace* our Redeemer. Since we can do all of the "right" things and not really know Him, I want us to consider what it's like to lunge face-first, arms wide open into an all-consuming relationship with God. A relationship that will transform every corner of our hearts!

REMEMBERING HE IS THERE, I CAN RELY ON HIM FOR WHATEVER I NEED IN EACH MOMENT— WHETHER IT IS WISDOM, INSIGHT, STRENGTH, LOVE, OR PATIENCE.

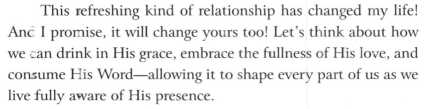

This refreshing kind of relationship has changed my life! And I promise, it will change yours too! Let's think about how we can drink in His grace, embrace the fullness of His love, and consume His Word—allowing it to shape every part of us as we live fully aware of His presence.

STRATEGIES TO EMBRACE YOUR REDEEMER

1. Drink in God's Grace

Every good thing in our lives is from God, and grace is one of the best gifts of all. He literally lavishes us with His grace! Read how Paul describes this truth to the church in Ephesus: "So we praise God for the glorious grace he has poured out on us who belong to his dear Son. He is so rich in kindness and grace that he purchased our freedom with the blood of his Son and forgave our sins. He has showered his kindness on us, along with all wisdom and understanding" (Eph.1:6–8, NLT). Amazing! God is so rich in kindness that He paid for our freedom with the blood of His Son! He poured out His "glorious grace" and "He has showered his kindness on us." It is up to us to drink it in, to soak it up. But how do we do that?

We can allow ourselves to be fully known by our grace-filled Redeemer. Because of His great kindness, we can completely trust Him with every part of our hearts, minds, and emotions. Since He knows us even better than we know ourselves, He is already aware of our every struggle. So why wouldn't we want to bring everything into His presence? When we do, we give Him the opportunity to redeem, restore, and renew every troubled spot!

UNDERSTANDING THE DEPTH OF HIS LOVE CALMS OUR FEARS, INCREASES OUR FAITH, STRENGTHENS OUR OBEDIENCE, AND ESCALATES OUR JOY!

Embracing God's grace isn't something we do one time, at the moment of salvation; we must do it continually. I don't know about you, but I need His grace in my thoughts, my fears, my insecurities, my doubts, my attitudes . . . well, some days that list seems endless. But understanding His kindness and grace helps me to know that I can invite Him into every one of those places. He longs to redeem anything I confess to Him.

I love the way *The Message* translates Psalm 103:8–14:

God is sheer mercy and grace;
not easily angered, he's rich in love.

He doesn't endlessly nag and scold,
nor hold grudges forever.
He doesn't treat us as our sins deserve,
nor pay us back in full for our wrongs.
As high as heaven is over the earth,
so strong is his love to those who fear him.
And as far as sunrise is from sunset,
he has separated us from our sins.
As parents feel for their children,
God feels for those who fear him.
He knows us inside and out,
keeps in mind that we're made of mud.

Understanding that God knows us completely, loves us thoroughly, and forgives us endlessly, should encourage us to fully embrace His grace. We do that every day as we bring our complete selves into His presence—even the ugly parts—and allow His mercy to remove our sins from us, "as far as the east is from the west" (Ps. 103:12).

Not only do we find forgiveness for our sins, we also discover His grace is sufficient for every need we have. When Mike and I were newly married we studied the Psalms together. The one thing that stood out to me from that particular study was the transparency of the psalmists. They shared the depths of their hearts with God. During that time I began to understand the principle of pouring my heart out to the Lord. When I fail to be transparent in His presence, I don't allow Him to help me with the things I face. The same is true for you. Transparency in prayer gives God the opportunity to meet you right where you are:

Are you exhausted? Tell Him; He is your rest.
(Ps. 62:1)

Are you full of anxiety? Tell Him; He is your peace.
(Ps. 34)

Are you overwhelmed with sorrow? Tell Him; He is your
comfort. (Ps. 119:76)

Are you weak? Tell Him; He is your strength.
(Ps. 28:6–8)

Are you needing direction? Tell Him; He is your guide.
(Ps. 32:8)

Are you empty? Tell Him; He is your portion.
(Ps. 63:1–5)

Are you brokenhearted? Tell Him; He wants to draw
you close. (Ps. 34:18)

Yes, my soul, find rest in God;
my hope comes from him.
Truly he is my rock and my salvation;
he is my fortress, I will not be shaken.
My salvation and my honor depend on God;
he is my mighty rock, my refuge.
Trust in him at all times, you people;
pour out your hearts to him,
for God is our refuge.
(PS. 62:5–8)

Let's drink in God's grace!

2. Receive the Fullness of God's Love

The song *Jesus Loves Me* is etched into my earliest childhood memories. I can remember wearing a white and black polka-dot dress with itchy lace, sitting in a small chair in the Beginners Sunday school classroom, and singing this simple song. Little did I know at the age of five, how those three words "Jesus loves me" would become the foundation of my life.

I've come to believe that embracing God's love is completely revolutionary—it absolutely changes us. Understanding the depth of His love calms our fears, increases our faith, strengthens our obedience, and escalates our joy! I've learned to trust His love even when my circumstances don't make sense and situations seem out of control.

Today, as I write this chapter my heart is so full of His encompassing love. And I want you to experience God's love in a fresh new way. Paul's prayer for the Ephesians is my prayer for you:

"I pray that from his glorious, unlimited resources he will empower you with inner strength through his Spirit. Then Christ will make his home in your hearts as you trust in him. Your roots will grow down into God's love and keep you strong. And may you have the power to understand, as all God's people should, how wide, how long, how high, and how deep his love is. May you experience the love of Christ, though it is too great to understand fully. Then you will be made complete with all the fullness of life and power that comes from God."

(EPH. 3:16–19, NLT)

27

If you are struggling to experience His love, I want to encourage you to read the "I am" statements of Jesus found in Appendix A and consider the love He displays for you in each verse. Let's receive the fullness of God's love!

3. Allow God's Word to Shape Your Thoughts, Attitudes, and Behaviors

Someone once said that the one time people read for all they're worth is when they're in love and are reading a love letter. That's the one time they read carefully and in depth!

My son Blake was out of the country for almost six months in 2008 with Youth With A Mission. He didn't have access to the Internet very often, and when he did, the connection usually wasn't strong enough for us to video chat. But several times we were able to send instant messages. Sometimes he would get access to the Internet when we couldn't chat, and he would send us a quick e-mail.

While these were not love letters per se, I missed our son so much that I simply devoured his notes. It's embarrassing to admit how many times I read Blake's e-mails. I read them at least three times immediately (not kidding) and would re-read them many times until we would hear from him again. The first time, I read an e-mail very quickly to make sure he was okay. Then I read it more slowly, looking closely at the details. I examined every phrase, looking for the emotion

THE BIBLE IS GOD'S WRITTEN REVELATION OF HIMSELF—THERE HE LONGS TO SHOW ME WHO HE IS, HOW HE SEES ME, AND WHAT IS BEST FOR MY LIFE.

behind the words—wondering if he was happy or overwhelmed. By the third time I read it, I could hear him saying the words and imagine the look on his face.

After considering how I read Blake's e-mails, I had to ask myself, do I read God's Word with the same intensity? Do I read every word—reflecting on what I learn about God and seeking to understand what He expects of me? Do I allow His Word to examine my motives and penetrate my thoughts and attitudes? Do I read it often enough to allow it to renew my mind?

I don't know about you, but many things try to influence my thoughts and attitudes. Sometimes difficult personal circumstances or the troubling situations in the world create anxiety. Sometimes disappointing relationships cause us to doubt. Even on the best days, life is full of difficulty. And when our focus is on what is happening around us, it shapes us more than we would like to admit. I'm not suggesting that we ignore our circumstances or live with our heads in the sand, but we can allow God's Word to bring us a different perspective—one that is life-giving.

When I read God's Word like a love letter, it changes the activity from a duty to check off my to-do-list to a time of intimate communication. The Bible is God's written revelation of Himself—there He longs to show me who He is, how He sees me, and what is best for my life. Only when I read it like a love letter can I allow it to penetrate my heart, adjust my thoughts, and realign my attitude. This time in His Word becomes the highlight of my day and overrides other things that try to shape my thoughts, attitudes, and behaviors.

So I want to encourage you to grab a cup of coffee (or tea, whatever is your favorite) and spend some time rereading

God's beautiful love letter. It will change you, I promise! Let's consume God's Word and allow it to define us!

4. Be Aware of God's Presence Every Moment

Sometimes the busy seasons of life leave us feeling frazzled and overwhelmed. In the midst of writing this book, I've been in a busy season of travel. I've had to remind myself daily to "practice the presence of God."

Let me explain. When I was in my twenties, someone gave me a copy of the book, *The Practice of the Presence of God*. It describes the journey of Brother Lawrence, a Frenchman who served as a cook in a seventeenth-century monastery. He wanted to live every moment with an overwhelming awareness of God's presence.

I've learned so much from this little book. Striving to be aware of God's presence has been absolutely life-changing for me. When I'm not living aware of God presence, I easily become distracted, frustrated, fearful, and overwhelmed with the responsibilities and cares of life. And my words and behaviors are always disappointing. (Remember my story of battling with Tyler!) However, when I make every effort to be aware of God's presence, my responses are completely different. Remembering He is there, I can rely on Him for whatever I need in each moment—whether it's wisdom, insight, strength, love, or patience.

I've learned from Brother Lawrence that you can have an ongoing "secret conversation of the soul" with God in the busiest moments. This is what others said about Brother Lawrence:

As Brother Lawrence had found such an advantage in walking in the presence of God, it was natural for him to recommend it earnestly to others; but his example was a stronger inducement than any arguments he could propose. His very countenance was edifying, such a sweet and calm devotion appearing in it as could not but affect the beholders. And it was observed that in the greatest hurry of business in the kitchen he still preserved his recollection and heavenly mindedness. He was never hasty nor loitering, but did each thing in its season, with an even, uninterrupted composure and tranquility of spirit. "The time of business," said he, "does not with me differ from the time of prayer, and in the noise and clatter of my kitchen, while several persons are at the same time calling for different things, I possess God in as great tranquility as if I were upon my knees [in prayer]." [2]

The first time I read *The Practice of the Presence of God*, I was a busy working mom of two active little boys. I discovered that I could make lunches and prepare for meetings in God's presence—believing He would help me every step of the way. It completely changed how I approached my day! I wanted to do everything with excellence. And I grew to depend on Him more every day. It was life-changing to remember that He was right there to give me everything I needed.

This truth is for us all—no matter what our day demands, we can grow to

OUR REDEEMER LONGS TO TEACH US WHAT IS BEST AND TO DIRECT US IN THE WAY WE SHOULD GO.

enjoy God's presence and possess the inner tranquility He offers. Let's strive to be aware of God's presence!

CONCLUSION

God created each of us as unique individuals, and He wants us to enjoy a *personal* relationship with Him. One of God's own traits is His desire for intimacy—to dwell with us and be known by us. In fact, the entire Bible is God's story of seeking to restore His relationship with mankind. From the following verses, we learn about the intimate relationship He desires to have with us:

- Psalm 56:8—He keeps track of every tear we cry.
- Psalm 62:8—He wants us to trust Him enough to pour out our hearts to Him.
- Psalm 63:7–8—He keeps us close to Himself for our protection.
- Psalm 139:1–4—He knows our every thought, word, and action.
- Psalm 139:17–18—He thinks about us constantly.

The Bible tells us about a man who had an extremely close relationship with God. His name was Enoch, and we really don't know much about him. Genesis 5 simply tells us he was the father of Methuselah, he walked faithfully with God, and then God took him. These are interesting facts, but not very insightful. The writer of Hebrews provides us with a little more information:

> By faith Enoch was taken from this life, so that he did not experience death: "He could not be found, because God had taken him away." For before he was taken, he was commended as one who pleased God. And without faith it is impossible to please God, because anyone who comes to him must believe that he exists and that he rewards those who earnestly seek him."
> (HEB. 11:5-6)

This passage describes Enoch as someone who pleased God. But we still don't know much about him. We don't know what Enoch's talents were or what he *did* for the Lord. Maybe those aren't included in his story because those aren't the things that please the Lord most! I wonder if these two passages tell us exactly what we need to learn from Enoch's life about pleasing God. First of all, we know Enoch believed God existed and sought Him with all of his heart. Secondly, we know all of his seeking led Enoch to "walk with God." This implies a close, personal, moment-by-moment relationship. Is this what God finds so pleasing?

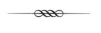

OUR REDEEMER HAS INVITED US TO RECEIVE HIS GRACE AND ENTER INTO A RELATIONSHIP WITH HIM THAT WILL POSITIVELY REVOLUTIONIZE OUR LIVES.

God's Word is full of promises for those who embrace Him, just like the one found in Hebrews 11—He "rewards those who earnestly seek Him." I want to renew my commitment to embrace Him for all I'm worth! I want to drink in His grace, embrace the fullness of His love, consume His Word—allowing it to shape every part of me—and live fully aware of His presence. My prayer for you is the same. May you be challenged in a fresh, new way today to a deeper relationship with our Redeemer!

GROUP DISCUSSION

1. Read through the definition of the word *redeemed* in the introduction and discuss what Christ offers us in His free gift of redemption.

   _____

   _____

   _____

   _____

   _____

   _____

   _____

2. Share your own story of redemption and your experience of God's grace with your group.

   _____

   _____

   _____

   _____

   _____

   _____

   _____

3. Read Psalm 103:8–14 together and discuss how understanding these truths can help us to be authentic in God's presence.

_____

_____

_____

_____

_____

_____

_____

_____

4. What hinders us from being authentic in God's presence?

_____

_____

_____

_____

_____

_____

_____

_____

5. Read together the "I am" statements of Jesus (found in Appendix A) and discuss all the ways Jesus displays His love for us. How can understanding the depth of His love change us?

_____

_____

_____

_____

_____

_____

_____

6. Read Psalm 19:7–14 together and list all the benefits of knowing God's Word found in this passage.

_____

_____

_____

_____

_____

_____

_____

_____

7. Read Galatians 5:16–26. Consider the emotional health of someone who allows her sinful nature to thrive. Contrast that with someone who is following the Holy Spirit's leading in every part of her life.

_____

_____

_____

_____

_____

_____

_____

_____

8. Share a time when you had an experience similar to mine with Tyler—where you felt the Holy Spirit guiding your words, attitudes, or a situation in your life.

_____

_____

_____

_____

_____

_____

_____

9. Share helpful ways for practicing the presence of God in everyday moments.

_____

_____

_____

_____

_____

_____

_____

_____

_____

10. I said, "God's Word is full of promises for those who embrace Him, just like the one found in Hebrews 11—He 'rewards those who earnestly seek Him.'" Share the ways you are challenged to embrace a relationship with God in fresh, new ways.

_____

_____

_____

_____

_____

_____

_____

DAILY READING, MEDITATION, & PRAYER

Chapter One: Embracing Our Redeemer

God works in our hearts as we read and meditate on His Word. Over the next five days, spend a few minutes every day allowing the truths you've discovered in chapter one to soak into your soul.

DAY 1

This is what the LORD says—your Redeemer, the Holy One of Israel: I am the LORD your God, who teaches you what is best for you, who directs you in the way you should go, If only you had paid attention to my commands, your peace would have been like a river, your well-being like the waves of the sea."

(ISA. 48:17–18)

Consider the peace and well-being that comes when you allow God to direct you. Thank God for the way He's led your life. Examine your heart to discover where you might need to seek His direction.

_____

_____

Dear God,

_____

_____

DAY 2

The LORD is gracious and compassionate,
slow to anger and rich in love.
The LORD is good to all;
he has compassion on all he has made.

(PS. 145:8–9)

Take time to thank God for His grace. Allow His grace to flood every corner of your heart.

_____

_____

_____

_____

_____

_____

Dear God,

_____

_____

_____

_____

_____

_____

_____

DAY 3

Jerusalem will be told: "Don't be afraid. Dear Zion, don't despair. Your God is present among you, a strong Warrior there to save you." Happy to have you back, he'll calm you with his love and delight you with his songs.

(ZEPH. 3:17, MSG)

Meditate on God's *great* love for you. Allow His love to encourage you!

_____

_____

_____

_____

_____

_____

_____

Dear God,

_____

_____

_____

_____

_____

_____

_____

DAY 4

I have hidden your word in my heart,
that I might not sin against you.
I praise you, O LORD; teach me your decrees.
I have recited aloud
all the regulations you have given us.
I have rejoiced in your laws
as much as in riches.
I will study your commandments
and reflect on your ways.
I will delight in your decrees
and not forget your word.

(PS. 119:11–16, NLT)

Consider the psalmist's love for God's Word. Consider all of the benefits of pursuing God's Word in this way.

_____

_____

_____

_____

Dear God,

_____

_____

_____

_____

DAY 5

Righteousness and justice are the foundation of your throne.
Unfailing love and truth walk before you as attendants.
Happy are those who hear the joyful call to worship,
for they will walk in the light of your presence, LORD.
They rejoice all day long in your wonderful reputation.
They exult in your righteousness.
You are their glorious strength.
It pleases you to make us strong.
Yes, our protection comes from the LORD,
and he, the Holy One of Israel, has given us our king.

(PS. 89:14–18, NLT)

Consider all of the benefits of walking in the light of God's presence.

_____

_____

_____

_____

_____

Dear God,

_____

_____

_____

_____

PERSONAL REFLECTION QUESTIONS

How does it make you feel when you realize the intimate relationship that God desires to have with you? Take some time to read these passages and reflect on His thoughts of you:

- Psalm 56:8—He keeps track of every tear you cry.
- Psalm 62:8—He desires for you to trust Him enough to pour out your heart to Him.
- Psalm 63:7–8—He keeps you close to Himself for your protection.
- Psalm 139:1–4—He knows your every thought, word, and action.
- Psalm 139:17–18—He thinks about you constantly.

Write out five ways God has revealed His love for you.

_____

_____

_____

_____

_____

_____

_____

_____

_____

_____

_____

_____

_____

_____

_____

_____

_____

_____

_____

_____

_____

_____

_____

I said, "Because of His great kindness, we can completely trust Him with every part of our hearts, minds, and emotions." What things do you find difficult to bring into God's presence? Take some time to search your heart and honestly bring those things to Him in prayer. Know that you can trust Him with every part of your life.

Take time to read Psalm 119. This chapter beautifully describes what it means to embrace God through His Word. Consider these ideas:

- Memorize it—Psalm 119:10–11
- Meditate on it— Psalm 119:15–16
- Pray it—Psalm 119:145–149
- Respond to it—Psalm 119:57–59
- Allow it to shape your thoughts and attitudes—Psalm 119:97–104

What has been your pattern for Bible reading in the last month? What new goals would you like to set and how will you keep them? How can you incorporate God's Word into your daily life?

_____

_____

_____

_____

_____

_____

_____

_____

_____

_____

_____

_____

What insights from the group discussion on practicing the presence of God were most helpful to you? Which suggestions can you incorporate immediately into your life? Which suggestions will take more time for you?

_____

_____

_____

_____

_____

_____

_____

_____

_____

_____

_____

_____

_____

_____

_____

_____

_____

_____

_____

_____

When do you feel that your sinful nature is the most in control? How can you allow the Holy Spirit to direct you in those specific moments?

_____

_____

_____

_____

_____

_____

_____

_____

_____

_____

_____

_____

_____

_____

_____

_____

_____

_____

_____

Write out the type of relationship you long to have with your Redeemer.

_____

_____

_____

_____

_____

_____

_____

_____

_____

_____

_____

_____

_____

_____

_____

_____

_____

_____

_____

_____

_____

_____

_____

_____

What steps can you take to embrace your Redeemer in a new way today? Remember, He rewards those who seek Him!

SCAN THIS CODE
WITH YOUR
·
SMARTPHONE
TO WATCH
A VIDEO
INTRODUCTION
TO THIS CHAPTER.

CHAPTER TWO

Redeeming Our Past

Praise the LORD, my soul,
and forget not all his benefits—
who forgives all your sins
and heals all your diseases,
who redeems your life from the pit
and crowns you with love and compassion,
who satisfies your desires with good things
so that your youth is renewed like the eagle's.
The LORD works righteousness
and justice for all the oppressed.
The LORD is compassionate and gracious,
slow to anger, abounding in love.
PSALM 103:2–6, 8

W hen my husband, Mike, and I served as pastors in Kansas, we met regularly with couples who needed counseling, but one situation broke our hearts in a significant way. I'll never forget the afternoon David and Mandy (names have been changed) walked into our office. They were a beautiful young couple who had started to attend our church. David explained the challenges they were experiencing. Then he asked Mandy to tell us a little about her background so we would understand their situation more fully.

With her eyes looking at the floor, Mandy told us how her father left the family and her parents divorced when she was very young. Her father was never a part of her life after he left. Shortly after the divorce, Mandy's mom fell into a deep depression and became addicted to prescription drugs. It wasn't long before her addiction turned to street drugs, and she started a relationship with a man who was involved in the same lifestyle. When Mandy was around twelve years old, her mom and the man she was with were unemployed and immersed in the drug culture. Many times they were unable to pay for their addiction, so they would take Mandy and offer her body to the dealers as payment for their drugs. These horrific transactions went on sporadically for several years.

> EVERY ONE OF US HAS A UNIQUE STORY, BUT WE ALL HAVE ONE THING IN COMMON—NO ONE ESCAPES THE NEGATIVE EFFECTS OF SIN!

When she was about fifteen years old, Mandy ran away to escape the nightmare she was living. Being too young for real employment, she had to lie about her age to get part-time jobs. She did whatever was necessary to survive. When she turned eighteen she got her GED and entered the work force. Through a series of life-altering events, Mandy met Jesus and surrendered her life completely to Him. Not long after that she met David, a strong Christian man. They fell in love and were married. While they both loved God and each other deeply, they faced many challenges in their marriage as a result of the scars in Mandy's heart.

As Mandy told us her story, it was so easy to envision her as a precious child and extremely difficult to imagine her being victimized in such a brutal way. Her parents were supposed to care for her and protect her—not sell her body for their drugs! As I sat listening to this precious woman's story, I could only imagine how these circumstances must have broken the heart of God!

It was never God's desire for Mandy to endure such suffering! But in His unfailing love, He brought her hope. Step by step, the redeeming process began to heal the broken places and restore what had been taken from her. Several years after the first conversation in our office, she stood in front of our congregation to share her story. Mandy wanted to help other victims of abuse and neglect experience healing as she had.

MY STORY AND YOURS

You may understand the heartaches of abuse all too well. Maybe you can relate to Mandy's story because it is a close reflection of your own journey. My story is very different from Mandy's. I was raised by Christian parents who worked hard to provide for me and tried their best to protect me from the damaging effects of sin. But the truth is, since Jesus is the only One who has lived a sinless life, no person was raised by perfect parents. And while my parents loved me, they were not able to protect me completely from the impact of sin. Every one of us has a unique story, but we all have one thing in common—no one escapes the negative effects of sin!

When I was growing up, neighbors were a consistent part of our daily lives. My brother and I knew all of the neighborhood kids. We rode bikes, played kickball in the street, climbed trees, ran through the sprinkler, and celebrated birthdays together. Oh, to be ten years old again . . . well, maybe not. I can't think about my childhood without remembering our neighborhood bully, Timmy Thompson (name changed). He taunted us continually. I don't think he ever called us by our names—he always used some cruel nickname made up to humiliate us. And he was so destructive; he was always breaking our things and picking fights. Since Timmy and I were in the same grade I felt like I could never escape his meanness. I can remember the absolute joy of finding out he wasn't in my class one year—I wanted to throw a party and invite everyone but Timmy! (I wasn't very mature in grade school.)

Thinking about Timmy now, I realize he was probably the recipient of cruelty in his own home, and his treatment of us was simply a reaction to the pain in his heart. Most children can't be that harsh without being provoked in some way. He may have treated us the way someone treated him.

I also remember the stomach-aches of my third grade year. I had full-blown nausea—the fear of my cruel teacher made me sick, literally. She was a master of humiliation and belittling. Today I can't remember her exact words, but I do remember how she made me feel. This was my first extremely negative experience with someone in authority over me. At the age of eight I didn't know how to handle this mistreatment, so my body responded with *real* tummy aches! I know my mom wasn't sure how to handle the situation. But, she believed the "sickness" was more emotional than physical, so she sent me to school and encouraged me to make the best of the situation. It was in third grade when I discovered adults can be as mean as Timmy Thompson. Each of us learns that lesson, and you may have learned it sooner than I did.

We all encounter sin's cruel manifestation as children. Whether we are sexually abused, like Mandy, had a cruel family life like Timmy, or we are the brunt of someone's cruel jokes, everyone has scars from the past. Since each of us is impacted by sin—you may have had someone who should have protected you but instead exposed you to things that were harmful. You may have had a parent who neglected you emotionally or physically. Maybe a teacher was cruel or a coach was belittling. A friend might have tried to ruin your reputation with vicious gossip. While I don't know the details of your story, I know that no one escapes the wounds of sin.

OUR CHOICES

As we grow from childhood into adolescence, every one of us makes choices we later regret. Whether we choose to lie, steal, gossip, or we neglect to do the good things we know we should do, we all sin. Each of our bad choices comes with corresponding consequences, and we can find ourselves in situations we would never choose. For example, if we lie, we will discover our relationships lack trust. We may even have the best of intentions, but every bad choice leads us down a path to some type of regret. In fact, all of our actions lead us to destinations. Author Andy Stanley in his book, *The Principle of the Path,* says, "At the end of the day, direction, not intention, determines destination." [3] Our actions are what count, and they are what determine the direction of our lives.

Our lives are impacted by the effects of sins—both the sins committed against us and the sins we have chosen for ourselves.

REDEMPTION

Salvation is not just a ticket to heaven, it's the opportunity to live fully restored from all of the baggage we carry around. Our pasts may not be forgotten and the effects of sin may linger, but the good news is the scars from the past can be redeemed! Jesus floods our lives with His grace and peace, and brings us the hope of a completely different future. Remember, we can't do anything to earn salvation. He loves us unconditionally and longs to cover us with His mercy. Once we accept this free gift, we can embrace His goodness and give Him the opportunity to heal the wounds of the past.

I don't want to oversimplify the healing process. In fact, many wounds may require the help of a godly, professional counselor. And healing may not come overnight. But as we spend time in God's presence, we give Him the opportunity to heal the scars. Consider these ideas:

STRATEGIES TO REDEEM YOUR PAST

1. Understand God's Ideal

One of the first steps to redeeming our past is to understand that these sinful, painful situations are not God's ideal for His children. The scars we carry are not because God is unkind or negligent in some way—the scars are a result of sinful humankind. When sin entered the world, the impact of sin came with it. And everyone is touched by the effects of sin. When we forget this truth, we find ourselves asking, "Where is God? How could He let this happen?" However, all the sin committed against us is not God's choice for us but the sinful choice of a person.

SALVATION IS NOT JUST A TICKET TO HEAVEN, IT IS THE OPPORTUNITY TO LIVE FULLY RESTORED FROM ALL OF THE BAGGAGE WE CARRY AROUND!

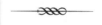

We see God's ideal for mankind in the account of creation and in the sinless life of Jesus. Before Adam and Eve chose to sin, they lived in a perfect world. They enjoyed a close, intimate relationship with one another and with God. Sin did not hinder their lives in any way—nothing was harmful, shameful, or hidden.

We also get a clear picture of God's character when we take a close look at the life of Jesus. Let's consider these words of Jesus to understand God's ideal treatment of children:

> "And whoever welcomes one such child in my name welcomes me. If anyone causes one of these little ones—those who believe in me—to stumble, it would be better for them to have a large millstone hung around their neck and to be drowned in the depths of the sea."
> (MATT. 18:5-6)

> "See that you do not despise one of these little ones. For I tell you that their angels in heaven always see the

face of my Father in heaven. What do you think? If a man owns a hundred sheep, and one of them wanders away, will he not leave the ninety-nine on the hills and go to look for the one that wandered off? And if he finds it, truly I tell you, he is happier about that one sheep than about the ninety-nine that did not wander off. In the same way your Father in heaven is not willing that any of these little ones should perish."

(MATT. 18:10–14)

I love these words of Jesus—we clearly see His love for children! We also learn more about the heart of God by observing how Jesus treated children. Remember, when Jesus lived here on earth, children were routinely excluded from adult settings and His own disciples saw them as a distraction. Read how He interacted with them, even when the disciples wanted Him to turn them away.

Then people brought little children to Jesus for him to place his hands on them and pray for them. But the disciples rebuked them. Jesus said, "Let the little children come to me, and do not hinder them, for the kingdom of heaven belongs to such as these." When he had placed his hands on them, he went on from there.

(MATT. 19:13–15)

Understanding God's ideal helps us to know that He weeps with every child who is wounded. When you were hurt, Jesus wept.

2. Embrace the Power of Forgiveness

The second part of redeeming our past is to embrace the power of forgiveness. Not only is each of us impacted by the sinful behavior of others, we too are guilty of sin. *Forgiveness*—it's something we all know we need. The good news is that Jesus freely offers us forgiveness and redemption. When He forgives us, He removes our sins, never to be remembered against us again.

Once we have received His grace, we must be willing to offer the same forgiveness to those who have sinned against us. In Matthew 6:14–15 Jesus tells His disciples they *must* forgive others. He even says if they don't forgive others, they won't be forgiven. I can only imagine how those who heard Jesus' words must have wondered about this challenging idea. It's obvious the apostle Peter thought about it and even wondered exactly what Jesus meant. Read this conversation between Peter and Jesus recorded in Matthew 18:21–35, NLT:

> Then Peter came to him and asked, "LORD, how often should I forgive someone who sins against me? Seven times?"
>
> "No, not seven times," Jesus replied, "but seventy times seven!
>
> "Therefore, the Kingdom of Heaven can be compared to a king who decided to bring his accounts up to date with servants who had borrowed money from him. In the process, one of his debtors was brought in who owed him millions of dollars. He couldn't pay, so his master ordered that he be sold—

along with his wife, his children, and everything he owned—to pay the debt.

"But the man fell down before his master and begged him, 'Please, be patient with me, and I will pay it all.' Then his master was filled with pity for him, and he released him and forgave his debt.

"But when the man left the king, he went to a fellow servant who owed him a few thousand dollars. He grabbed him by the throat and demanded instant payment.

"His fellow servant fell down before him and begged for a little more time. 'Be patient with me, and I will pay it,' he pleaded. But his creditor wouldn't wait. He had the man arrested and put in prison until the debt could be paid in full.

"When some of the other servants saw this, they were very upset. They went to the king and told him everything that had happened. Then the king called in the man he had forgiven and said, 'You evil servant! I forgave you that tremendous debt because you pleaded with me. Shouldn't you have mercy on your fellow servant, just as I had mercy on you?' Then the angry king sent the man to prison to be tortured until he had paid his entire debt.

"That's what my heavenly Father will do to you if you refuse to forgive your brothers and sisters from your heart."

Jesus taught that if we really understand the depth of God's forgiveness of our sin, we will forgive others. We may feel our sin is nothing compared to the sin that has been committed against us, but each of us is guilty in the eyes of our *perfect* Redeemer. And He paid our debt completely, a debt we could never pay.

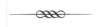

ALL THE SIN COMMITTED AGAINST US IS NOT GOD'S CHOICE FOR US BUT THE SINFUL CHOICE OF A PERSON!

The truth is, it isn't easy to forgive others. We can even have misconceptions about what forgiveness really is, which makes it even harder. I remember a time when someone hurt our family deeply. I knew I needed to forgive her, but it seemed impossible. After all, she didn't even ask for forgiveness. Every time I saw the person who hurt us, I would get a sick feeling in the pit of my stomach. Then I would think, *If I've really forgiven her, I shouldn't feel this way about her.*

What I didn't understand was that forgiveness isn't a *feeling*. The pain of the event was real, and the negative feelings were the appropriate response to the situation. Bad feelings are not wrong. Jesus experienced negative emotions—He felt sorrow, disappointment, and anger. But He didn't allow His feelings to cause Him to sin. And, yes, refusing to forgive is sin.

Let's consider this a little more. If forgiveness isn't a feeling, what is it? Here are a few thoughts about forgiveness:

1. Forgiveness *is not* pretending nothing happened.
2. Forgiveness *is not* unconditional trust and maintaining the relationship as it was before the offense.
3. Forgiveness *is not* condoning someone's sinful behavior.

4. Forgiveness *is* choosing not to retaliate or get even.
5. Forgiveness *is* choosing to give good to the one who has harmed us instead of the evil that person has given to us.
6. Forgiveness *is* ongoing and might include setting healthy boundaries.

Ultimately, forgiveness is a choice. A close friend told me, "You can never *feel* your way into right behaviors, but you can *behave* your way into right feelings." She was helping me to understand that if we allow our feelings to lead our lives, our negative feelings will bring wrong behaviors and negative attitudes. But when we choose to be obedient and respond appropriately in spite of our negative feelings, our feelings will eventually get better.

I've found this principle to be true. If I allow negative feelings to control my responses by talking about the person or trying to get even, bitterness settles into my heart. This bitterness doesn't hurt the person who has offended me, but it harms me in so many ways. I continually relive the pain and experience the situation over and over again.

My inability to forgive others also hinders my relationship with God. Resentment against others builds a wall between God and me. I'm basically taking matters into my own hands, wanting vengeance and immediate justice to be done to the one who has offended me. God wants to be my advocate, my protector, and my Redeemer, but when I hold on to situations I'm not allowing Him to take care of the situation or me. Forgiveness gives me the opportunity to be free from a situation and to completely trust God with the outcome.

I'm so thankful that we don't have to be slaves to our feelings, but we can *behave* our way into right feelings! We must choose to be obedient and forgive; we must choose not to get even and to give good instead of evil. These behaviors reveal our confidence in God as our avenger, and they directly impact our emotions. Right responses begin to lessen the pain. However, our feelings may not change overnight; I want to encourage you to be patient with the process. (If you're struggling to forgive those who have hurt you, you may want to seek the help of a professional Christian counselor. Many times the outside perspective a counselor offers to a person brings healing to that situation.)

Forgiveness is freeing! It removes the impact of the sin committed against us and allows us to walk in the redemption Christ offers us.

3. Celebrate Those Who Have Brought You Healing

We should celebrate the redeeming relationships God brings into our life journeys. He uses people to bring hope and healing. Sometimes redemption comes through the simple act of kindness by a complete stranger, and other times He places someone strategically in our lives for a season.

Many individuals have played an important role in my life. I clearly remember Janie Steiner, my ninth-grade English teacher. Janie is a follower of Jesus, and she made a dramatic impact on me. Unlike my harsh, cruel teacher in third grade, my relationship with Miss Steiner was redemptive. I'm sure you will agree . . . junior high school can be absolutely horrific! I remember struggling with all kinds of insecure thoughts, but

Miss Steiner extended God's redeeming love and acceptance during this pivotal time in my life. She spoke such encouraging words to me. I distinctly remember her telling me how she believed I had God-given leadership potential. She thought I was intelligent and had something to offer. She encouraged me towards leadership positions and urged me to do my best in every endeavor. God strategically placed her in my life to challenge me in the right direction. I know my high school experience was dramatically impacted by her positive influence. How thankful I am for the redemptive work Christ brought to my life through Miss Steiner!

Think about the people God has strategically placed in your life to love and encourage you. Celebrate them! Be thankful for them.

4. Offer Redemption to Others, Especially Children

The final step in redeeming our past is to offer God's ideal treatment to the children in our lives. Not all of us have children of our own, but every woman was created uniquely to bear and nurture children. By design, you have the ability to leave deep impressions on children. Someone said, "People may not remember what you say, but they will remember how you made them *feel*." As I think back to the women I encountered as a child, distinct feelings arise with each one. Some memories are definitely not pleasant, but others bring warmth, acceptance, and encouragement.

WHEN YOU WERE HURT, JESUS WEPT!

The children in your family, neighborhood, and church are impacted by the effects of sin every day. But you can bring redemption to them with words of affirmation and encouragement. Every child, like Mae Mobley in the movie *The He'p,* needs an Aibileen to say to her, "You is kind. You is smart. You is important." Who is the "Mae Mobley" in your life? How can you offer that child redemption?

CONCLUSION

The effects of sin have negatively impacted each of us—it is the result of living in a fallen world. God's ideal plan never included sin. But since He created us with the ability to choose, there will always be those who decide to sin. Sin consistently brings consequences, but one of the most beautiful things about redemption is the way God's grace restores and renews those things sin robs from us. Romans 8:28 tells us that God works all things together for our good. This includes the sins committed against us, and the sins we have committed. What a beautiful gift He offers us in this passage—He can take our broken lives and make them whole!

Jesus quoted from this Isaiah passage, telling His audience that He was the fulfillment of this prophecy. Read it carefully and note all of the ways He redeems our past:

"The Spirit of the Sovereign LORD is on me, because the LORD has anointed me to proclaim good news to the poor. He has sent me to bind up the brokenhearted, to proclaim freedom for the captives and release from darkness for the prisoners, to proclaim the year of the LORD's favor and the day of vengeance of our

God, to comfort all who mourn, and provide for those who grieve in Zion—to bestow on them a crown of beauty instead of ashes, the oil of joy instead of mourning, and a garment of praise instead of a spirit of despair. They will be called oaks of righteousness, a planting of the LORD for the display of his splendor."
(ISA. 61:1–3)

Salvation is a free gift—a gift we receive when we humbly repent of our sin and acknowledge Jesus as our Savior. But accepting salvation is simply the first step in a lifelong journey with our Creator. He wants to redeem our past and heal the scars that sin has left in our hearts. He doesn't want us to live beneath the pain and suffering of sin, but this part of the redemptive process requires our involvement. We should:

1. Remember that sin is never God's ideal plan for us—He weeps when we are sinned against. We can trust His love for us!
2. Forgive. God forgives us—removing our sins as far as the east is from the west, never to be remembered against us again. And we must offer the same forgiveness to those who have harmed us. Bitterness keeps us tied to the pain, but forgiveness sets us free!
3. Celebrate those who have shared God's redemptive plan and encouraging words with us.
4. Offer God's redeeming grace to those around us, especially children.

The last phrase of Isaiah 61:3 says, "They will be called oaks of righteousness, a planting of the LORD for the display of his splendor." Just think about that for a moment. Your redeemed life displays the splendor of God!

GROUP DISCUSSION

1. I said that even godly parents can't completely protect their children from the effects of sin. Why is this true?

_____

_____

_____

_____

_____

_____

2. How important is it for us to remember that sin is a choice people make, it is not God's ideal? How does that knowledge help the one who was abused as a child?

_____

_____

_____

_____

_____

_____

_____

3. Hebrews 12:15 encourages us to, "See to it that no one misses the grace of God and that no bitter root grows up to cause trouble and defile many." How does bitterness "cause trouble and defile many"?

_____

_____

_____

_____

_____

_____

_____

4. God's commands are always for our good. Describe how offering forgiveness to those who have sinned against us is good for us. How is forgiveness freeing?

_____

_____

_____

_____

_____

_____

_____

_____

_____

5. Share with the group an example of an adult who positively influenced you.

_____

_____

_____

_____

_____

_____

_____

_____

6. Psalm 103:2–5 speaks of God redeeming our past. Read those verses aloud using several translations, and examine it together phrase by phrase.

_____

_____

_____

_____

_____

_____

_____

_____

_____

7. Read Isaiah 61:1–3 and note all the ways God wants to redeem the hurts from our past.

_____

_____

_____

_____

_____

_____

_____

_____

DAILY READING,
MEDITATION, & PRAYER

Chapter Two: Redeeming Our Past

God works in our hearts as we read and meditate on His Word. Over the next five days, spend a few minutes every day allowing the truths you've discovered in chapter two to soak into your soul.

DAY 1

Praise the LORD, my soul,
and forget not all his benefits—
who forgives all your sins
and heals all your diseases,
who redeems your life from the pit
and crowns you with love and compassion,
who satisfies your desires with good things
so that your youth is renewed like the eagle's.
The LORD works righteousness
and justice for all the oppressed.
The LORD is compassionate and gracious,
slow to anger, abounding in love.

(PS. 103:2–6, 8)

Consider all of the Lord's benefits. Thank Him for all the times He has forgiven you, healed you, redeemed you from the effects of sin, revealed His love, and satisfied your desires.

_____

_____

_____

_____

_____

_____

_____

_____

Dear God,

_____

_____

_____

_____

_____

_____

_____

_____

_____

DAY 2

You keep track of all my sorrows.
You have collected all my tears in your bottle.
You have recorded each one in your book.

(PS. 56:8, NLT)

How do you feel when you realize that God cares about every tear you shed? Thank Him for understanding your sorrow.

_____

_____

_____

_____

_____

_____

Dear God,

_____

_____

_____

_____

_____

_____

_____

DAY 3

If we confess our sins, he is faithful and just and will forgive us
our sins and purify us from all unrighteousness.

(1 JOHN 1:9)

Thank God for His forgiveness. Ask Him to fill your heart with the
joy of forgiveness.

_____

_____

_____

_____

_____

_____

Dear God,

_____

_____

_____

_____

_____

_____

DAY 4

Every time I think of you, I give thanks to my God. Whenever I pray, I make my requests for all of you with joy, for you have been my partners in spreading the Good News about Christ from the time you first heard it until now. And I am certain that God, who began the good work within you, will continue his work until it is finally finished on the day when Christ Jesus returns.

(PHIL. 1:3-6, NLT)

Spend some time thanking God for the people He has used to bring you healing and hope.

_____

_____

_____

_____

_____

_____

Dear God,

_____

_____

_____

_____

_____

_____

DAY 5

Therefore encourage one another and build each other up . . .
(1 THESS. 5:11)

Consider the young people God has placed in your life. Ask the Lord
to show you creative ways to encourage them.

_____

_____

_____

_____

_____

_____

_____

_____

Dear God,

_____

_____

_____

_____

_____

_____

_____

PERSONAL REFLECTION QUESTIONS

What are the scars from your childhood? How have you allowed God to redeem and restore those situations? Are there still situations you need to take into His presence and allow Him to heal?

_____

_____

_____

_____

_____

_____

_____

_____

_____

_____

_____

_____

_____

_____

_____

_____

_____

Read this psalm David wrote when the Philistines were attacking him (Ps. 56, NLT):

> *O God, have mercy on me,*
> *for people are hounding me.*
> *My foes attack me all day long.*
> *I am constantly hounded by those who slander me,*
> *and many are boldly attacking me.*
> *But when I am afraid,*
> *I will put my trust in you.*
> *I praise God for what he has promised.*
> *I trust in God, so why should I be afraid?*
> *What can mere mortals do to me?*
> *They are always twisting what I say;*
> *they spend their days plotting to harm me.*
> *They come together to spy on me—*
> *watching my every step, eager to kill me.*
> *Don't let them get away with their wickedness;*
> *in your anger, O God, bring them down.*
> *You keep track of all my sorrows*
> *You have collected all my tears in your bottle.*
> *You have recorded each one in your book.*
> *My enemies will retreat when I call to you for help.*
> *This I know: God is on my side!*
> *I praise God for what he has promised;*
> *yes, I praise the LORD for what he has promised.*
> *I trust in God, so why should I be afraid?*
> *What can mere mortals do to me?*
> *I will fulfill my vows to you, O God,*
> *and will offer a sacrifice of thanks for your help.*

(CONTINUED)

For you have rescued me from death;
you have kept my feet from slipping.
So now I can walk in your presence, O God,
in your life-giving light.

How do you feel when you remember that it was not God's ideal plan for you to be harmed in any way?

_____

_____

_____

_____

_____

_____

_____

_____

_____

_____

_____

_____

_____

_____

Reread pages 65–66 that discuss what forgiveness is and what it isn't. How have you misunderstood forgiveness? Are there people you need to forgive? What steps should you take?

Which individuals can you celebrate for bringing God's redemptive plan into your life? Take some time today to express your appreciation to one of them.

Who are the children in your life? Ask God to help you know how to offer redemption to them through the words you speak and the things you do with them. Commit to redeeming relationships with all of the children in your sphere of influence.

SCAN THIS CODE
WITH YOUR
SMARTPHONE
TO WATCH
A VIDEO
INTRODUCTION
TO THIS CHAPTER.

CHAPTER THREE

Redeeming Our Perspective

Do not fear, for I have redeemed you;
I have summoned you by name; you are mine.

ISAIAH 43:1

I will never forget the moment Mike and I found out we
were going to be grandparents. Tyler and Katie (our son
and daughter-in-law) asked us to go out for a late dinner on a
Wednesday night after church. We went to one of our favorite
brick-oven pizza places in Wichita. I was sitting in the booth
directly across from Katie, when she slid a card across the table
to us. They had just returned from being out of town, and
while they were gone we had "dog sat" Tino (our cute little
grand-dog) for them. Since Katie is really good about giving
cards, my immediate thought was, *how considerate—a thank-you
note.* I was not at all anticipating the announcement the card
was about to deliver.

Once I had the card in my hands I noticed the look on their faces. Obviously, the card was more than a thank-you note. As I was opening it, Tyler asked me to read it out loud so his dad could hear it too. *Wow, it is so important that he wants us to hear it at the same time? What on earth?* I was still clueless, until I read the first four words . . . some of the sweetest words on earth.

Dear Grandma and Grandpa,
My mom and dad just found out that I'm on my way.
And we wanted you to know, too. I love you so much
and I can't wait to meet you in September!
Baby

I could hardly read after the "Dear Grandma and Grandpa." The huge lump in my throat was making it difficult to speak. But Mike and I were saying at the same time, "What!? Really!? You're pregnant!?" Immediately, everyone around the table was wiping tears from their eyes. *Wow, our kids are going to be parents.* We were ecstatic! Since we were in a restaurant I had to suppress the scream of delight I wanted to let out. (If the truth be known, Tyler and Katie probably asked us to a public place to make the announcement so I would contain my enthusiasm at an appropriate level.)

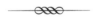

NOT ONLY WAS GOD INVOLVED IN OUR CREATION, HE IS INTIMATELY ATTENTIVE TO US RIGHT NOW.

If I thought it was wonderful to hear that a baby was on the way, getting to see the sonogram that told us she was a girl was even better. And better still was the amazing gift of being in the room when Molly Jayne was born! (Did I mention that I have a great daughter-in-law? Katie allowed me to be with her during labor *and* delivery. Since I don't have a daughter of my own, God gave me the best daughter-in-law a mother could ever ask for.)

The sight of Molly's little newborn face will be etched on my heart forever. Nothing is more precious! Unless it's the sound of her little two-year-old voice saying, "I'm *Grammy's* girl, no . . . I'm *Papa's* girl." Both statements couldn't be more accurate. She is *our* girl!

From the moment I read that Molly Jayne was on her way, I loved her more than I can describe. Why? Simply because she belongs to us! She is my child's child. Quite honestly she didn't have to do *anything* to earn my love. I was praying for her years before she was even conceived. And since that Wednesday night, a day hasn't passed without thinking about our sweet Molly.

YOU BELONG TO GOD

Some people believe that God created Adam and Eve and then let nature take its course, implying we are all born as a random act of biology. Believing this idea is devaluing to each of us. It diminishes the sanctity of all human life. But Psalm 139 beautifully depicts that God carefully made each one of us, watched us while we were still in our mothers' wombs, planned our days, thinks about us, and is constantly present with us.

> You made all the delicate, inner parts of my body
> and knit me together in my mother's womb.
> Thank you for making me so wonderfully complex!
> Your workmanship is marvelous—how well I know it.

You watched me as I was being formed in utter seclusion,
as I was woven together in the dark of the womb.
You saw me before I was born.
Every day of my life was recorded in your book.
Every moment was laid out
before a single day had passed.
How precious are your thoughts about me, O God.
They cannot be numbered!
I can't even count them;
they outnumber the grains of sand!
And when I wake up,
you are still with me!
(PS. 139:13–18, NLT)

How awesome is that? It doesn't sound very random to me,
does it to you? Not only was God involved in our creation, He is
intimately attentive to us right now. Verses one through five of
that same chapter describe God's on-going awareness of us.

O Lord, you have examined my heart
and know everything about me.
You know when I sit down or stand up.
You know my thoughts even when I'm far away.
You see me when I travel
and when I rest at home.
You know everything I do.
You know what I am going to say
even before I say it, Lord.
You go before me and follow me.
You place your hand of blessing on my head.

You belong to God! As His child, God's love for you and His attention to your life is even greater than the affection of a new grandma!

REDEMPTION

A few days after Molly was born, I read the book of Deuteronomy. Chapter six struck me in an entirely different way as a new grandma. Moses encouraged the people to love God, to live by His guidelines, and to think about His goodness. Then he admonished them to talk about all of these things with their children and grandchildren.

I immediately began thinking about the things I wanted my life to teach Molly. Maybe God allows us to have grandparents so they can share a perspective that can only be gained with time and experience. I can think of several things I want my children and grandchildren to know. At the top

HE NOT ONLY MADE YOU, BUT HE SUSTAINS YOU, DEFINES YOU, CARES FOR YOU, ACCEPTS YOU, AND DESIGNED YOU FOR A SPECIFIC PURPOSE.

of the list is a lesson that took me a long time to discover— the right perspective of who I am and what actually brings fulfillment to life.

Many things will potentially influence the way Molly views herself. For instance, our modern, American culture is obsessed with youthful, sex-appealing bodies. Today, perhaps more than any time in the past few centuries, women and girls are obsessed with their physical appearance. A book entitled *The Body Project* shares insights gained from reading young women's journals (ages fourteen through thirty years old) from the Victorian age through today. The earliest journals were full of character issues and descriptions of the young women's faith. They spoke about their affections for their family members and friends. But today, young women's journals are full of the way they feel about their bodies and their ability to attract guys. Most of them never mention issues of character, faith, or family. [4]

YOU ARE WONDERFULLY COMPLEX, AND NO ONE ELSE CAN BE YOU!

Others may try to tell Molly that education defines who she is and what she can become. Education is important, and we want to develop the natural gifts and talents God places in our lives. But if we allow education to become more than good stewardship of the gifts we are given, we can have an over-inflated view of ourselves and believe we are self-made. Right behind those beliefs is the lure of positions, power, and possessions—defining ourselves by what we accomplish.

Some women allow the men in their lives to define them—they base their value on the type of man who is attracted to them. Still others feel defined by their talents or a perceived lack of talents. None of these perspectives is the accurate lens with which to view ourselves.

- If we think a sexy body gives us value, the natural aging process will destroy our self-worth; our pursuits will become shallow and self-absorbed.
- If positions define us, our perceived value is diminished with every challenge and job change.

- If we think power will actually empower us, we will claw our way to the top—and find ourselves completely alone.
- If we expect a man to bring us security, identity, acceptance, and purpose, we will live frustrated and unfilled lives because no man can bring what only God is capable of giving us.
- If we believe our talents create our value, we will constantly compare ourselves to others and clamor for ways to make ourselves seem better.

I want Molly, *and you,* to embrace a redeeming, life-altering perspective. The right perspective starts by believing that you belong to God. He not only made you, but He sustains you, defines you, cares for you, accepts you, and designed you for a specific purpose.

Let's consider some ideas to help us redeem our perspective.

STRATEGIES TO REDEEM YOUR PERSPECTIVE

1. Allow God to Define You

Once when I was having lunch with my wise friend Peggy Musgrove (you met her in the Introduction), I asked her what advice she would most want to offer young Christian women. Her immediate response was, "Allow God to define you. Don't compare yourselves to others; instead allow the Holy Spirit to lead you." What great advice!

First of all, God created each of us individually. He places us in a specific time in history and location in the world. He designs us with a unique set of strengths and a distinct personality. You are wonderfully complex, and no one else can be you!

Comparisons aren't good for our hearts. The conclusions we make when we compare ourselves to others lead us to unhealthy attitudes like pride *(I'm better)*, discouragement *(I'll never measure up)*, discontentment *(if only I had ___ like her, I could ___)*, or jealousy *(I wish I was more like them)*. None of these perspectives encourages our souls or leads us in a good direction.

The good news is you don't have to compare yourself to anyone. You weren't made to be anyone other than you. You were designed to be *you*. However, this isn't an excuse to ignore your negative characteristics and stop growing. (I once heard a woman say, "I have a temper. That's the way I am—everyone just needs to deal with that." By the way, she has alienated almost everyone in her life.) We all need our character to be refined. This is part of God's plan for us. He wants us to continually grow and become more like Christ.

Comparisons keep us focused in the wrong direction, and so do self-centered attitudes. Self-absorbed thoughts cause us to focus on what we *think* is lacking in our lives. These thoughts are despairing—and tend to keep us even more self-centered. This negative cycle causes us to be consumed with our comfort and selfish desires and to neglect our character and emotional maturity.

We can't allow God to define us if we're comparing ourselves to others or if we're self-absorbed. The right perspective comes when we choose to be God-focused. As we obediently allow

Him to lead every part of our lives, we will discover our true selves—the women He created us to be. We can trust His love and discover that His definition of each one of us is much greater than anything we could ever write for ourselves.

2. Find Your Security in God

So many things can cause us to feel anxious—the world's current economic state, foreign affairs, the unemployment rate, the stability of our own employment, crime, or even the frailty of human life (just to name a few). God doesn't want us to live with these anxieties. His Word tells us that embracing His love brings the right perspective and drives away all fear.

COMPARISONS KEEP US FOCUSED IN THE WRONG DIRECTION, AND SO DO SELF-CENTERED ATTITUDES.

The psalmist David is described as a man after God's own heart. We get a glimpse of the close relationship he had with God by reading through his psalms. David absolutely believed God created him, knew him, loved him, and would *sustain* him. Throughout the psalms we find verses David penned to thank God for His great care and protection. Just like the psalmist, God wants us to find our security in Him. Read through these verses and consider the security you can have:

> But let all who take refuge in you rejoice;
> let them sing joyful praises forever.
> Spread your protection over them,
> that all who love your name may be filled with joy.
> For you bless the godly, O LORD;

you surround them with your shield of love.

(PS. 5:11–12, NLT)

Everyone who honors your name
can trust you,
because you are faithful
to all who depend on you.

(PS. 9:10, CEV)

The LORD is my light and my salvation—
so why should I be afraid?
The LORD is my fortress, protecting me from danger,
so why should I tremble?

(PS. 27:1, NLT)

Where can I go from your Spirit?
Where can I flee from your presence?
If I go up to the heavens, you are there;
if I make my bed in the depths, you are there.
If I rise on the wings of the dawn,
if I settle on the far side of the sea,
even there your hand will guide me,
your right hand will hold me fast.

(PS. 139:7–10)

Allow the truths of those verses to sink deep into your
heart. You can trust God completely.

3. Accept Your Limitations

When God created life He established some non-negotiable limitations. For instance, no matter how much we want to stretch time, we only get twenty-four hours a day. He created us with physical limitations—we all need nourishment and rest. And there is a

limit to our resources, our energy, *and* our abilities. We are even limited in the number of meaningful relationships we can enjoy at one time.

Some seasons of life have built-in limitations—such as lack of experience for the young, limited time for new parents, and diminished strength in times of illness. This is a simple truth of our human existence.

In one of my favorite books, *Strengthening the Soul of Your Leadership,* author Ruth Haley Barton shares an eye-opening truth about living within our limits:

When we refuse to live within limits, we are refusing to live with a basic reality of human existence. . . . Our unwillingness to live within limits is one of the deepest sources of depletion and eventual burnout. . . . Living graciously within the boundaries of our life as it has been entrusted to us gives our life substance. Oddly enough, something of the will of God is contained in the very limits that we often try to sidestep or ignore.

Living with limits is not in any way an acquiescence that is despairing, passive or fatalistic. Rather it honors the deepest realities of the life God has given us. [5]

I haven't always lived submissively within my limits. But as I reflect on my life, I can see a distinct pattern. When I ignore my natural limitations, I get out of balance and it affects my productivity, my relationships, my emotional health, and my physical strength. However, when I honor those limitations, I'm actually more productive, content in my relationships, and healthier.

We aren't designed to do it all! Remember that "the will of God is contained in the very limits that we often try to sidestep or ignore." This perspective will help us to live graciously and most productively within our God-ordained limits.

4. Stop Longing for the Ideal

A couple of years ago Mike and I faced a life-changing decision—we could say no, or we could say yes. There really wasn't a third option. The first option was to say no to the new opportunity we felt God had prepared specifically for us and stay where we were. Or we could say yes to the open door, which would require us to leave our family and friends. One afternoon as I was considering the options, I distinctly remember thinking, *neither choice is ideal!* No matter what decision we made, the outcome would

I'VE DISCOVERED THAT WHEN I'M NOT DEMANDING *IDEAL* CIRCUMSTANCES, MY HEART CAN REST IN GOD'S *IDEAL* LOVE.

be less than perfect. Disheartening, right? I went to bed that night completely discouraged.

I'm amazed at the gentle, loving way God corrected my perspective. The next morning I was reading *The Relationship Principles of Jesus,* by Tom Holladay, a devotional book divided into forty readings. That day's section was entitled "Get Rid of the Ideal, Go for the Real." Holladay said we can make an idol out of the *ideal.* What a sobering truth! Immediately I realized that was exactly what I had done—I had made myself miserable by longing for the "ideal." It was as if I thought we needed perfect circumstances to find contentment and fulfillment.

Holladay challenged his readers,

The circumstances of your life are not perfect. You are not perfect. The people you love are not perfect. But God is perfect. So instead of trying to perfect the imperfectable, choose to focus on praising the one who is perfect. And then, bolstered by that praise, choose real love. [6]

Needless to say, I had to repent. I had spent too much time longing for an idyllic life. It was such a good reminder that our circumstances on earth will *never be ideal!* If we don't manage those unrealistic expectations they will create discontentment, discouragement, frustration, and ingratitude.

In the end, Mike and I made the decision to walk through the door we felt God had opened for us. We tearfully said good-bye to many dear friends, our young adult children, and one precious grandbaby (definitely not ideal!). I still miss them terribly. But, I've discovered that when I'm not demanding *ideal* circumstances, my heart can rest in God's *ideal* love. And then, bolstered by His love, the despair flees, and I can live with humble dependence and joyful gratitude.

5. Embrace God's Purpose for Your Life

Most of life is work. We spend the majority of our time working at our jobs, working in our homes, and doing things for other people. God created us this way—to serve others. But if we don't have a right perspective of work, we can become embittered against the things we "have to do." Since serving is a part of our design, we can find our greatest fulfillment and joy as we discover our purpose and embrace the work we are given to do.

God had plans for our lives even before we were born (Ps. 139:16). You were created on purpose and with a purpose. The apostle Paul says it this way, "For we are God's handiwork, created in Christ Jesus to do good works, which God prepared in advance for us to do" (Eph. 2:10).

Even the account of creation describes the work we are to do—

> God spoke: "Let us make human beings in our image,
> make them reflecting our nature
> So they can be responsible for the fish in the sea,
> the birds in the air, the cattle,
> And, yes, Earth itself,
> and every animal that moves on the face of Earth."
> God created human beings;
> he created them godlike,
> Reflecting God's nature.

He created them male and female.
God blessed them:
"Prosper! Reproduce! Fill Earth! Take charge!
Be responsible for fish in the sea and birds in the air,
for every living thing that moves on the face of Earth."
(GEN. 1:26–28, MSG)

We are created in God's image—and since He works, work has always been a part of God's plan for our lives. This mandate was actually given *before* sin entered the world—work is not a result of the curse. God designed humankind to have dominion over and to manage His creation. Because sin and deterioration entered the world, our work also includes restorative, redemptive work.

WE AREN'T
DESIGNED
TO DO IT ALL!

Some people think that only those involved in Christian ministries are a part of God's redemptive purposes on earth. But let's consider how all honorable work fulfills God's plan for people to expand and maintain life.

- Law enforcement officers, corrections officers, attorneys, and judges work to protect and maintain order.
- Housekeepers and custodians restore cleanliness and bring order to homes, public buildings, and work places.
- Architects, construction workers, plumbers, electricians, landscapers, and designers create and maintain homes that are needed for shelter and protection.

- Healthcare providers work to maintain and restore the wellness of their patients.
- Mechanics work to restore things that are broken.
- Educators invest in the lives of their students— helping them to grow and develop.
- Those who work in farming or food services help to meet the physical needs of people.
- The work of hair stylists, clothing retailers, and other merchants provides various services and resources everyone needs.
- Engineers, researchers, and scientists work to make life better.
- Musicians and artists reflect God's beauty and help us express the emotions in our hearts.
- Financial planners, accountants, help us manage our resources appropriately.
- Counselors, advisors, and life coaches help others to grow and maintain healthy perspectives.
- Writers and publishers help to inform and share knowledge.

We can easily understand the difference between jobs that are honorable and those that are not. Work that harms and exploits others—pornography, theft, prostitution, illegal drugs—is directly opposed to God's redemptive plan. Since we're told to love and serve others, we can be assured that our work will in some way benefit people. "Our people must learn to devote themselves to doing

YOU WERE CREATED ON PURPOSE AND WITH A PURPOSE.

what is good, in order to provide for urgent needs and not live unproductive lives" (Titus 3:14).

As we discover and develop the natural gifts God has given to us, He will open the right doors of opportunity designed specifically for us. When we do every task (even the smallest, seemingly insignificant ones) to the best of our abilities and work as if we are working for Christ, God blesses our work and gives us more opportunities and leads us to greater fulfillment.

So, let's not fall into a consumer mindset—one that desires to be served and to accumulate things. While this is a lure of fleshly desires, it's a shallow, unfulfilling way to live. We'll find our purpose and our greatest satisfaction when we take our eyes off of ourselves and serve others. Many parents and grandparents experience this joy when a new baby comes into their lives. New babies require complete care—we have to carry them, feed them, bathe them, clothe them, and wipe their noses and their bottoms. Yet the fulfillment we discover in caring for them can't be compared to any other task we have. Why? Because we're most fulfilled when we live for others. I was struck with this reality when I read the Facebook status of my sweet friend, Andrea.

Andrea Wells FB status 8.14.12
My house isn't perfectly clean, like it used to be. The laundry always seems to be spilling out of the hamper. Our floors are littered with bright, colorful tripping hazards. We are usually up by 6am on the weekends . . . but we are greeted by a big smile and lots of hugs. I haven't gone to the bathroom by myself in months. I have worn (and inadvertently tasted) human feces. I

have succumbed to a schedule based around sleeping, pooping, eating, and lots of playing and cuddling. I was terrified I would lose myself and my freedom . . . but the last year I have truly found myself and my purpose. And in the last year I have discovered a new depth of freedom and joy. Psalm 127:3. This has been the best year of our lives. Happy 1st Birthday Wren Juliette!! [7]

CONCLUSION

The right perspective begins when I know that I'm not a random act of nature—I'm lovingly and attentively designed by God. He created me to be a unique and specific part of His redemptive work on earth. The first step to discover His plan for my life is to accept the redeeming grace of His Son, Jesus. I will discover His plan as I keep my focus on Him, and allow His Word to shape me into the woman He designed me to be. I can find security in the knowledge that He will provide and care for me every day of my life. I don't have to be Super Woman; I can live humbly within my God-given limitations and discover His perfect will for my life (limits and all). When I demand *ideal* circumstances, I waste mental energy and create unhealthy emotions—I should focus on God's *real* loving provisions with gratitude. When I develop the gifts He has placed in my life and seize the opportunities He gives me, with a genuine desire to serve, I find my greatest fulfillment. I become the woman He created me to be.

GROUP DISCUSSION

1. Discuss the difference in knowing you are lovingly and attentively created by God versus thinking you are a random act of biology.

_____

_____

_____

_____

_____

_____

_____

2. Read through the unhealthy perspectives of self-worth found on pages 94–95. Discuss the ways our culture teaches these ideas and the pitfalls of viewing ourselves through these lenses.

_____

_____

_____

_____

_____

_____

_____

3. Since God created us, it only makes sense to allow Him to help us grow into the women He designed us to be. How can comparing ourselves to others hinder our growth?

_____

_____

_____

_____

_____

_____

_____

4. How can self-centered attitudes cause us to neglect our emotional health and character development?

_____

_____

_____

_____

_____

_____

_____

5. Read through the verses that describe God's care. Discuss the ways we can replace our anxieties with the knowledge of God's love and provision.

_____

_____

_____

_____

_____

_____

6. Describe what happens when people try to live beyond their God-given limitations. How can this cause burnout and discouragement? What happens when we live graciously within our limitations?

_____

_____

_____

_____

_____

_____

_____

_____

7. Read the quote from Tom Holladay's book *The Relationship Principles of Jesus* on page 101. Describe some examples of people trying to "perfect the imperfectable." How can longing for the ideal create unhealthy emotions?

_____

_____

_____

_____

_____

_____

_____

_____

8. What happens to our attitudes when we embrace God's *real* love and trust Him with our less than ideal circumstances?

_____

_____

_____

_____

_____

_____

_____

9. Tell the group one way you serve others and bring restoration to the world around you. (It can be as simple as picking up after your children.) Then discuss the importance of having the right perspective of the work assigned to us.

_____

_____

_____

_____

_____

_____

_____

_____

10. Read the conclusion together and make a commitment to strive for healthy perspectives.

_____

_____

_____

_____

_____

_____

_____

DAILY READING, MEDITATION, & PRAYER

Chapter Three: Redeeming Our Perspective

God works in our hearts as we read and meditate on His Word. Over the next five days, spend a few minutes every day allowing the truths you've discovered in chapter three to soak into your soul.

DAY 1

You made all the delicate, inner parts of my body
and knit me together in my mother's womb.
Thank you for making me so wonderfully complex!
Your workmanship is marvelous—how well I know it.
You watched me as I was being formed in utter seclusion,
as I was woven together in the dark of the womb.
You saw me before I was born.
Every day of my life was recorded in your book.
Every moment was laid out
before a single day had passed.
How precious are your thoughts about me, O God.
They cannot be numbered!
I can't even count them;
they outnumber the grains of sand!
And when I wake up,
you are still with me!

(PS. 139:13–18, NLT)

Read each verse slowly and allow the truth of each phrase to sink into your heart. Then consider why you should allow God to define you.

_____

_____

_____

_____

_____

_____

_____

_____

Dear God,

_____

_____

_____

_____

_____

_____

_____

_____

_____

_____

DAY 2

Whoever dwells in the shelter of the Most High
will rest in the shadow of the Almighty.
I will say of the LORD, "He is my refuge and my fortress,
my God, in whom I trust."
Surely he will save you
from the fowler's snare
and from the deadly pestilence.
He will cover you with his feathers,
and under his wings you will find refuge;
his faithfulness will be your shield and rampart.
You will not fear the terror of night,
nor the arrow that flies by day,
nor the pestilence that stalks in the darkness,
nor the plague that destroys at midday.
A thousand may fall at your side,
ten thousand at your right hand,
but it will not come near you.
You will only observe with your eyes
and see the punishment of the wicked.
If you say, "The LORD is my refuge,"
and you make the Most High your dwelling,
no harm will overtake you,
no disaster will come near your tent.
For he will command his angels concerning you
to guard you in all your ways.

(PS. 91:1–11)

Read each verse slowly and allow the provision of the Lord to encompass every anxiety in your heart.

_____

_____

_____

_____

_____

_____

_____

_____

_____

Dear God,

_____

_____

_____

_____

_____

_____

_____

_____

DAY 3

As a father has compassion on his children,
so the L<small>ORD</small> has compassion on those who fear him;
for he knows how we are formed,
he remembers that we are dust.
The life of mortals is like grass,
they flourish like a flower of the field;

(PS. 103:13–15)

Consider how God made us and knows our every limitation. Let this realization bring you peace.

_____

_____

_____

_____

_____

_____

Dear God,

_____

_____

_____

_____

_____

DAY 4

Therefore do not worry about tomorrow, for tomorrow will worry about itself. Each day has enough trouble of its own.

(MATT. 6:34)

Jesus told us this life wouldn't be ideal. Consider how we can experience peace as we let go of the longing for an ideal life.

_____

_____

_____

_____

_____

_____

Dear God,

_____

_____

_____

_____

_____

_____

DAY 5

Work willingly at whatever you do, as though you were working for the LORD rather than for people. Remember that the LORD will give you an inheritance as your reward, and that the Master you are serving is Christ.

(COL. 3:23–24, NLT)

Consider how you can work today as if Jesus were standing beside you in the flesh.

_____

_____

_____

_____

_____

_____

Dear God,

_____

_____

_____

_____

_____

_____

_____

PERSONAL REFLECTION QUESTIONS

Read through the section "You Belong to Him" and write out how it makes you feel to know that God loving and attentively made you.

_____

_____

_____

_____

_____

_____

_____

_____

_____

_____

_____

_____

_____

_____

_____

_____

_____

_____

What have you allowed to define you? What steps do you need to take to allow God to shape you into the woman He created you to be?

_____

_____

_____

_____

_____

_____

_____

_____

_____

_____

_____

_____

_____

_____

_____

_____

_____

_____

_____

_____

_____

_____

Where are you most insecure? Find a passage of Scripture that describes God's care for you in that particular area and memorize it. (You can use the "keyword search" feature at www.biblegateway.com to find a verse.)

_____

_____

_____

_____

_____

_____

_____

_____

_____

_____

_____

_____

_____

_____

_____

_____

_____

When are you most tempted to push beyond your God-given limits? How can you embrace them instead? Describe the freedom that can be experienced when you accept your limits.

_____

_____

_____

_____

_____

_____

_____

_____

_____

_____

_____

_____

_____

_____

_____

_____

_____

_____

_____

Take an honest look at your attitudes. When do you find yourself longing for the ideal? How can you accept the real and trust God's love with the "less than perfect" parts of your life?

Do you ever find yourself grumbling about the work in your life? How can you adjust your perspectives to live fully for God's purposes? How can you do every task with excellence and for His honor? Are you faithful in the little things, or are you negligent in what seems insignificant?

Read through the conclusion, then write your own commitment to have the right perspective of yourself and the work God has given you to do.

SCAN THIS CODE
WITH YOUR
SMARTPHONE
TO WATCH
A VIDEO
INTRODUCTION
TO THIS CHAPTER.

Redeeming Our Sexuality

In you, O LORD, I have taken refuge;
let me never be put to shame;
deliver me in your righteousness.
Free me from the trap that is set for me,
for you are my refuge.
Into your hands I commit my spirit;
redeem me, O LORD, the God of truth.

PSALM 31:1, 4–5, NIV 1984

R ecently, I had dinner with a long-time friend. (I'm not as young as I think I am. This reality hits me every time I talk to a friend from my teenage years, and I realize just how *long* we've known each other!) She and I live in different cities so we don't get to see each other very often; it was great to catch up! We made a lot of good memories when we were younger, and we had a solid group of friends from church who were a part of those memories. As we "walked down memory lane"

IT'S IMPORTANT
FOR US TO RUN
TO GOD NOT
AWAY FROM HIM.

we began to realize just how many of our friends are divorced, almost all of them as a result of unfaithfulness. We also have several friends who live a homosexual lifestyle or who deal with other gender identity issues. It was disheartening to think about the painful situations those friends have encountered.

Since I decided to write this book, the Lord has led me to several situations that made me feel the pain many women face regarding their sexuality. I've talked with missionaries who work with sex trafficking victims. The plight of these women and girls is more devastating than you can imagine. I've studied Islam and ministered to Muslim women in Europe. The male domination of Islamic cultures creates an environment for many abuses. While I was in Latin America, I heard the story of a young girl whose mother placed drugs in her vagina and sent her out into dangerous streets to deliver those drugs. Here in the United States "mommy porn" is currently on the best-seller list, and sexually explicit movies targeting women are mainstream entertainment.

My heart is *extremely* heavy as I consider the ways women and girls are wounded by these situations. The sad reality is—many of us carry sexual offenses. Some wounds are deeper than others, but all of them are painful. I've been privileged to serve in girls' and women's ministries for more than two decades. It's an absolute joy to know and to be a part of so many women's lives, but through the years I've heard dozens and dozens of painful stories caused by:

- **Exposure**—many young girls are exposed to
  sexual images, conversations, and encounters
  long before they're able to make well-informed
  decisions about their sexuality. Even as adults, we
  can be unwittingly exposed to things we would
  never want in our thoughts by simply overhearing
  a conversation or seeing a provocative image.
- **Early experimentation**—when young girls have
  been prematurely exposed to sexual issues, some
  of them experiment at an early age.
- **Objectification** (viewing women as sexual
  objects)—many women receive unwanted sexual
  advances at school and in the workplace.
- **Exploitation**—the number of ways women
  are exploited sexually is daunting: abuse, rape,
  stalking, sex trafficking, incest, pornography,
  and prostitution. The statistics on rape alone are
  staggering. "An exhaustive government survey
  of rape and domestic violence released [in
  December 2011] affirmed that sexual violence
  against women remains endemic in the United
  States and in some instances may be far more
  common than previously thought. Nearly one in
  five women surveyed said they had been raped or
  had experienced an attempted rape at some point,
  and one in four reported having been beaten by
  an intimate partner. One in six women have been
  stalked, according to the report." [8]

- **Incest**—it's always devastating, but the closer the relative and the greater frequency of the events, the more harmful and lasting the negative effects.
- **Gender identity**—homosexuality, bisexuality, and transgender issues are becoming more mainstream and impacting women's lives.
- **Promiscuity/adultery**—some women, even Christian woman, buy into the popular views of our culture and find themselves making poor sexual choices.
- **Unfaithfulness of a spouse**—some women remain sexually pure but are negatively impacted by the adulterous choices of their husbands.
- **Unhealthy sexual practices within marriage**—one or both spouses become addicted to pornography, sex toys, or fetishes. (These practices are always unfulfilling and create distance between a husband and wife). Other couples allow unresolved relational issues to separate them sexually.

REDEMPTION

Sadly, only a few of us have not been impacted by at least one of these issues. The scars on our souls are deep—it seems the wounds sexual sins leave behind are different from any other kind of wound. *The Message* translation of 1 Corinthians 6:16–20 helps us to understand why:

There's more to sex than mere skin on skin. Sex is as much spiritual mystery as physical fact. As written in

Scripture, "The two become one." Since we want to become spiritually one with the Master, we must not pursue the kind of sex that avoids commitment and intimacy, leaving us more lonely than ever—the kind of sex that can never "become one." There is a sense in which sexual sins are different from all others. In sexual sin we violate the sacredness of our own bodies, these bodies that were made for God-given and God-modeled love, for "becoming one" with another. Or didn't you realize that your body is a sacred place, the place of the Holy Spirit? Don't you see that you can't live however you please, squandering what God paid such a high price for? The physical part of you is not some piece of property belonging to the spiritual part of you. God owns the whole works. So let people see God in and through your body.

Like all other sins, sexual sin is not God's ideal for His daughters. Our pain and brokenness break His heart. It's why Christ died. He longs to bring healing, forgiveness, and wholeness.

STRATEGIES TO REDEEM YOUR SEXUALITY

1. Understand that Sexual Sin Is Not the "Unforgivable Sin" and Receive God's Forgiveness

No matter where we find ourselves, as the victim of sexual exploitation or as the woman who has chosen sexual sin, the shame associated with either situation is real. If we want to know what God's response is to the one who is involved in sexual sin, we can read Jesus' response to the woman who was caught in adultery:

> As he was speaking, the teachers of religious law and the Pharisees brought a woman who had been caught in the act of adultery. They put her in front of the crowd.
>
> "Teacher," they said to Jesus, "this woman was caught in the act of adultery. The law of Moses says to stone her. What do you say?"
>
> They were trying to trap him into saying something they could use against him, but Jesus stooped down and wrote in the dust with his finger. They kept demanding an answer, so he stood up again and said, "All right, but let the one who has never sinned throw the first stone!" Then he stooped down again and wrote in the dust.
>
> When the accusers heard this, they slipped away one by one, beginning with the oldest, until only Jesus was left in the middle of the crowd with the woman. Then Jesus stood up again and said to the woman, "Where are your accusers? Didn't even one of them condemn you?"
>
> "No, Lord," she said.
>
> And Jesus said, "Neither do I. Go and sin no more."
>
> (JOHN 8:3–11, NLT)

Jesus doesn't condemn us, nor does He see us as "damaged goods." When Jesus said, "Let the one who has never sinned throw the first stone," He was helping us to see that sin is sin.

As with all sin, He lovingly offers forgiveness and the power to choose differently.

He longs to remove the shame and restore the joy of a pure heart. The Bible describes David, a great king in the Old Testament, as "a man after God's own heart," yet he committed adultery with a woman named Bathsheba. After Nathan confronted David about his sin, David prayed this prayer of repentance. (Notice how he asked God to help him have pure thoughts and a faithful heart.)

"A psalm by David when the prophet Nathan came to him after David had been with Bathsheba."

You are kind, God!
Please have pity on me.
You are always merciful!
Please wipe away my sins.
Wash me clean from all
of my sin and guilt.
I know about my sins,
and I cannot forget my terrible guilt.
You are really the one
I have sinned against;
I have disobeyed you
and have done wrong.
So it is right and fair for you
to correct and punish me.
I have sinned and done wrong
since the day I was born.
But you want complete honesty,

so teach me true wisdom.
Wash me with hyssop
until I am clean and whiter than snow.
Let me be happy and joyful!
You crushed my bones,
now let them celebrate.
Turn your eyes from my sin
and cover my guilt.
Create pure thoughts in me
and make me faithful again.
Don't chase me away from you
or take your Holy Spirit
away from me.
Make me as happy as you did
when you saved me;
make me want to obey!

(PS. 51:1–12, CEV)

When we feel overwhelmed with the shame of sexual sin, we want to hide—which causes us to withdraw from our relationship with God. But it's important for us to run *to* God not *away* from Him. He will not reject us. God's forgiveness not only removes our feeling of shame, He chooses never to hold our sin against us. He redeems us by washing us and making us whiter than snow! He gives us joy and helps us to have pure thoughts and a desire for faithfulness. Since He forgives us, we can forgive ourselves!

Do you remember the strategies we shared in chapter one for embracing our Redeemer? As we continue to pursue an intimate relationship with Him, He will continue to heal and restore all of the brokenness that sexual sin has left in our hearts. He wants to redeem our past (Chapter 2) and our perspectives completely (Chapter 3). We can live free from sexual sin!

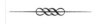

GOD IS THE CREATOR OF LIFE, AND HE KNOWS THE BEST WAY TO LIVE IT.

2. Know How to Respond to Unhealthy Cultural Trends

God created us as sexual beings; it's a part of who we are. God created a woman to enjoy physical intimacy with her husband. But in our over-sexualized culture, we can be lured into many unbiblical thoughts about our sexuality. Let's consider a few of these cultural lies:

- Sex is all about me!
- Sex is just sex; it doesn't impact any other part of my life.
- It doesn't matter who I have sex with, or how many different people I have sex with.
- Pornography, sex toys, and fetishes are all okay in a consenting relationship. If it feels good, do it.

God is the Creator of life, and He knows the best way to live it. He gave His Word for our benefit. Following His plan in the expression of sexuality brings health to our relationships and joy to our hearts. The enemy of our souls would like for us to believe these cultural lies and fall into destructive patterns that will only destroy our relationships and steal our joy. "The thief's purpose is to steal and kill and destroy. My purpose is to give them a rich and satisfying life" (John 10:10, NLT).

So what does God's Word say about those cultural ideas? It is *not* all about me! Sexual intimacy is all about relationship and *selflessness*. A wife should always come to the marriage bed looking to fulfill her husband and to grow closer to him—giving herself to him and pursuing intimacy with him. Real intimacy and fulfillment are found when *each* partner takes an "it's not about me" attitude and looks to please his or her spouse.

> The husband should fulfill his marital duty to his wife, and likewise the wife to her husband. The wife's body does not belong to her alone but also to her husband. In the same way, the husband's body does not belong to him alone but also to his wife. Do not deprive each other except by mutual consent and for a time, so that you may devote yourselves to prayer.
> (1 COR. 7:3–5, NIV 1984)

Sexual sin impacts a woman deeply; that's why it matters deeply who she has sex with!

Earlier we read 1 Corinthians 6:16–20, a passage that helps us to understand how sexual sin violates the sacredness of our own bodies. The passage below warns us against having sex with someone who is not our spouse.

> God's will is for you to be holy, so stay away from all sexual sin. Then each of you will control his own

body and live in holiness and honor—not in lustful passion like the pagans who do not know God and his ways. Never harm or cheat a Christian brother in this matter by violating his wife, for the LORD avenges all such sins, as we have solemnly warned you before. God has called us to live holy lives, not impure lives. Therefore, anyone who refuses to live by these rules is not disobeying human teaching but is rejecting God, who gives his Holy Spirit to you.

(1 THESS. 4:3–8, NLT)

Pornography, sex toys, fetishes, and role playing diminish intimacy. Many people think toys and pornography are the answer to diminishing sexual interest in one another. But according to Dr. Jim Vigil, the opposite is true:

External tools cannot replace a genuine pursuit of knowing the other. . . . Usually those external tools and toys are made to enhance the sexual experience. The danger in this is that the focus becomes the ecstasy brought on by mechanics rather than by genuine intimate relationship. The mechanics can be impersonal and lead to self-centeredness. Not only is psychological self-centeredness present, but also a neurological distortion occurs. . . . When a person has a sexual release, the brain experiences a release of chemicals called endorphins and encephalins—the highest rush in the human body. Cocaine affects this same area of the brain, which is why cocaine is so addictive. Because the effect of the chemical release is brought on through a specific behavior, the person will continue the practice. When a person experiences the "high," whatever else he or she is experiencing at the time (whether it is a partner, pornography, prostitution, sex devices, or fetishes) becomes fused with the experience–a bonding occurs. So if a person has a sexual fantasy, he or she will start bonding to that fantasy world; if pornography, pornography becomes that fulfillment; if through masturbation, the person begins to equate sexual fulfillment with himself or herself—not with his or her spouse. The fantasies, devices, and practices will become the objects of desire—rather than the person bonding to his or her spouse. [9]

God wants a woman to associate sexual release with her husband—bonding the two of them and nurturing true intimacy. (He wants a woman to be "addicted" to her husband! That's really cool!) Sex devices, pornography, and masturbation will never bring true fulfillment nor will they foster intimacy. Additionally, because of the physiological responses, sexual addictions can be the most difficult to break—which is why the apostle Paul tells us that sexual sins are so damaging: "Run away from sexual sin! No other sin so clearly affects the body as this one does. For sexual immorality is a sin against your own body" (1 Cor. 6:18, NLT).

If we dress up or role-play as another personality, we open the door for our husbands to fantasize about being with someone else. Why would we want to be responsible for planting thoughts that could potentially tempt our husbands to be with another woman? We should want to keep our body and attire attractive for our husbands, but our lingerie should help them focus on us, rather than on a fantasy. And as a wife, each woman should make love to her husband, not to someone in a fantasy world. Sexual role-playing opens doors that are better left closed. "Whatever is true . . . whatever is right, whatever is pure . . . think about such things" (Phil. 4:8).

Knowing God's Word will help us to respond appropriately to the unhealthy sexual trends in society. Sadly, those modern thoughts and practices are leading women down a path that ends in brokenness. However, following God's design will lead us to pure intimacy and greater fulfillment.

3. Establish Healthy Personal Boundaries

Whether we are married or single, we should establish some healthy personal boundaries to help us live according to God's will. (Remember, following His will doesn't diminish our fulfillment, it increases it!) Here are a few of the boundaries I have found helpful.

Guard your heart! When Mike and I were first married, I watched soap operas just about every day. I found myself comparing Mike to the men on the shows. (I know this is really shallow, but confession is good for the soul!) Either I didn't think he was living up to the romantic displays of the good guys; or I was worried he

REMEMBER, FOLLOWING HIS WILL DOESN'T DIMINISH OUR FULFILLMENT, IT INCREASES IT!

would do some horrible thing like the bad guys. Wow, how unhealthy is that? So I decided to stop watching soap operas. A few years later, I discovered that I shouldn't read romance novels as well. They do the same thing—they open the wrong doors in my thoughts. I committed to these boundaries because Mike is really awesome and he shouldn't have to compete with *fictional characters!* (Life isn't a fairy tale! No one is married to Prince Charming!)

Because of past experiences and individual design, each of us has personal areas of vulnerability. We need to be aware of the activities or situations that tempt us to fantasize about other men, to be dissatisfied with our husbands, to criticize our appearance, or to feel unhappy about our sex lives. So let's guard our hearts! If the magazines we read, the movies we watch, or the music we listen to creates dissatisfaction, let's make a good decision and stop allowing that "stuff" into our hearts and minds. We can ask God to help us set appropriate boundaries and pray this prayer:

> Look deep into my heart, God, and find out everything I am thinking. Don't let me follow evil ways, but lead me in the way that time has proven true.
> (PS. 139:23–24, CEV)

Avoid inappropriate conversations with friends! We may also need to set a personal boundary in our conversations with friends. Many women talk openly about the details of their sex lives. This is a common but harmful reality of our society. These discussions shouldn't be a part of healthy friendships among women. Sexual intimacy is designed for *exclusivity.*

Only then can a husband and wife experience complete and total trust, complete and total freedom, and complete and total fulfillment. A woman should guard her husband and the intimacy she shares with him. Additionally, when we discuss our sex lives with our friends, we're tempting them to have sexual thoughts about our husbands. (If a couple needs counseling for the sexual issues of their marriage, they can talk together with a mentor or counselor.)

> But among you there must not be even a hint of sexual immorality, or of any kind of impurity, or of greed, because these are improper for God's holy people. Nor should there be obscenity, foolish talk or coarse joking, which are out of place, but rather thanksgiving.
>
> (EPH. 5:3-4)

Don't let the flame die! (This one is just for wives.) When we're newly married we can't imagine our desire for sexual intimacy ever waning. But, it's a great idea to pray that *we'll always desire our husband's touch.* If we've been married for many years and our desire for intimacy has diminished over time, or if past experiences have negatively impacted this area of our marriage, God is more than able to heal and restore sexual desire and fulfillment. Ask God to help you desire and enjoy pure sexual intimacy with your husband (or *future* husband, for all you single ladies). Don't simply pray and wait for the feelings to return.

WHEN WE DISCUSS OUR SEX LIVES WITH OUR FRIENDS, WE'RE TEMPTING THEM TO HAVE SEXUAL THOUGHTS ABOUT OUR HUSBANDS.

Pray and then pursue your husband with a selfless desire to bring him fulfillment—God will honor your selflessness. "May you rejoice in the [husband] of your youth . . . may you ever be captivated by [his] love" (Prov. 5:18–19).

4. Don't Get too Close to Another Man

Friends, we can't forget that we have an enemy who would like nothing more than to destroy our lives with sexual sin. Whether we are single, newly married, or have been married for decades, we need to respond immediately to the signs that we're getting too close to a man who is not our husband (if we're married) or a married man (if we're single). Here are the warning signs to watch for:

Internal Warning Signs: *Do I . . .*
- dress with him in mind?
- feel heightened excitement when he is around?
- compare my husband to him? (if married)
- desire to spend time alone with him?
- secretly hope that he will notice me?
- feel the need to impress or please him?
- think of him often throughout the day?

External Warning Signs: *Do either he or I . . .*
- give excessive compliments to each other?
- show affection beyond gestures of friendship?
- exchange gifts?
- spend time alone together?
- discuss sexual topics?

- talk about our hurts, frustrations, or feelings when spouses are not present?
- feel as though conversation should be guarded when spouses are present?
- get upset when spouses seems to interfere with our relationship?

Immediately heed these warning signs. If any of these apply to you, take aggressive action to move your heart, mind, and actions in the opposite direction! (In other words—get away from the guy! Fast) We can never be too careful when protecting our hearts and our relationships!

Guard your heart above all else,
for it determines the course of your life.
Avoid all perverse talk;
stay away from corrupt speech.
Look straight ahead,
and fix your eyes on what lies before you.
Mark out a straight path for your feet;
stay on the safe path.
Don't get sidetracked;
keep your feet from following evil.
(PROV. 4:23–27, NLT)

5. Respect Men

How we interact with men says a lot about our hearts. I just read a Facebook post that said: "MEN ARE DUMB IDIOTS." (Yes, it was all in caps.) I've no idea what circumstances led this woman to post such a strong comment, but it makes me sad that she is so full of resentment. You see, I believe the way we respond to people is a direct reflection of the condition of our own hearts. My Facebook friend's statement says much more about what is going on inside of her than the intellectual capacity of men.

Yes, it's true, some men take advantage of us. Some of them abuse and mistreat us. And we need to be wise—we should never put ourselves in harm's way! As much as possible, we should remove ourselves from men who are dangerous. Friend, if you're single and dating a man who mistreats you in *any* way, *run!* I can guarantee you that things will not get better after you're married. When people are dating, they always put their best foot forward. If your boyfriend doesn't treat you with respect and care now, it will only get worse after you say, "I do." Being single is much better than living with an abusive man! Be patient and wait for a wonderful, godly man who will cherish you and treat you with respect.

> WE NEED TO BE AWARE OF THE ACTIVITIES OR SITUATIONS THAT TEMPT US TO FANTASIZE ABOUT OTHER MEN.

Even if we have had negative experiences, or we haven't found the right man to share our lives with, we need to remember that God instructs us to, "Show proper respect to everyone" (1 Pet. 2:17). When we choose to show others respect, we reveal the quality of our character. It really has nothing to do with the worthiness of the person to whom we show respect.

Have you ever thought about the respect and dignity Christ showed to individuals? Think about the woman who was caught in adultery, tax collectors who were known for swindling, children who were clamoring for His attention, Pilate who questioned Him, religious leaders who despised Him, close friends who abandoned Him, and even the soldiers who killed Him. Christ was able to interact respectfully with these individuals because of who He was. He never allowed the negative behavior of someone else to change who He was. He didn't act disrespectfully because someone was unworthy of respect—even when He was mistreated and despised. Quite honestly, the dignity He gave to them was a direct reflection of His impeccable character.

The same is true for us. The respect or disrespect we give to others is an outward expression of *our* inner character and strength. When we find ourselves being disrespectful or unkind to men, we should ask ourselves what is at the center of our behavior. Sometimes we're disrespectful because men fail to live up to our expectations. We may want them to validate us or meet other deep needs they're not equipped to meet. Since God made us, we should allow Him to define us and bring us worth (see Chapter 3). Only He can meet the deepest needs in our hearts.

WHEN WE CHOOSE TO SHOW OTHERS RESPECT, WE REVEAL THE QUALITY OF OUR CHARACTER.

Single women, have you ever considered how flirting with a man who is married is a form of disrespect? We should never entice a man to sin. There is no such thing as "harmless flirting" with a married man. Married women, have you ever considered how flirting with any man, other than your husband, is disrespectful to your marriage covenant, yourself, and your husband? Flirting with the wrong man is a disrespectful activity that opens dangerous doors.

Men don't define us—God does. Men can't meet our deepest needs—only God can. We don't have to allow men to use us—we can choose to live by God's standards. We don't flirt with men or dress provocatively to entice men because we respect ourselves. We can have healthy, respectful relationships with men because we are redeemed!

CONCLUSION

Many of us have been victims of abuse or have been exposed to perversion, which steals our joy and makes wholeness feel like a distant dream. Others have chosen immoral lifestyles, which always distorts our view of purity. But God's redeeming grace reaches to the depths of who we are and completely sets us free from the emotional, mental, and physical strongholds of sexual sin!

The forgiveness God gives happens instantaneously, but restoration is usually a process that requires our participation. As we continually receive His mercy, He removes our shame and doesn't hold our sin against us. We need to allow His truth to displace the ideas of our culture or the distorted views caused by abuse or promiscuity. Healthy boundaries will help us live obediently within His will. We also need to respond immediately to the warning signs that we are getting close to any man other than our husband. And finally, since we are redeemed, we can show respect to men and live our lives without the slightest hint of sexual inappropriateness.

God's redeeming grace and transforming work give us the privilege of knowing the joy of sexual purity!

GROUP DISCUSSION

1. Discuss the general messages of current movies and popular books regarding sexuality. How do these ideas contradict or confirm biblical ideas?

_____

_____

_____

_____

_____

_____

_____

2. Read 1 Corinthians 6:16–20 and discuss the ways sexual sin affects us differently than other sin.

_____

_____

_____

_____

_____

_____

_____

3. Sexual sin may have a greater impact on our hearts, but it is not a greater sin than other sins in the eyes of God. What is the importance of embracing this truth (for the one who has sinned, and for the way we view those who commit sexual sin)?

_____

_____

_____

_____

_____

_____

4. Discuss the ways we can guard our hearts against the lies of cultural sexual trends.

_____

_____

_____

_____

_____

_____

_____

5. I shared a few personal boundaries I use to guard my heart. Share with the group some boundaries you have found helpful.

6. As a group, write a description of a healthy relationship with a man who is not your husband.

7. Considering all of the verses in this chapter and the insights I gave, discuss the ways we can encourage a friend who has been sexually abused. What about a repentant friend who has committed sexual sin?

_____

_____

_____

_____

_____

_____

_____

8. Share the insight from this chapter that stands out the most to you.

_____

_____

_____

_____

_____

_____

_____

_____

DAILY READING, MEDITATION, & PRAYER

Chapter Four: Redeeming Our Sexuality

God works in our hearts as we read and meditate on His Word. Over the next five days, spend a few minutes every day allowing the truths you've discovered in chapter four to soak into your soul.

DAY 1

Purify me from my sins, and I will be clean;
wash me, and I will be whiter than snow.
Oh, give me back my joy again;
you have broken me—
now let me rejoice.
Don't keep looking at my sins.
Remove the stain of my guilt.
Create in me a clean heart, O God.
Renew a loyal spirit within me.

(PS. 51:7–10, NLT)

Read each verse slowly and allow the truth of each phrase to sink into your heart. Then thank God for removing your guilt and shame.

_____

_____

_____

_____

_____

_____

_____

_____

Dear God,

_____

_____

_____

_____

_____

_____

_____

_____

DAY 2

There's more to sex than mere skin on skin. Sex is as much spiritual mystery as physical fact. As written in Scripture, "The two become one." Since we want to become spiritually one with the Master, we must not pursue the kind of sex that avoids commitment and intimacy, leaving us more lonely than ever—the kind of sex that can never "become one." There is a sense in which sexual sins are different from all others. In sexual sin we violate the sacredness of our own bodies, these bodies that were made for God-given and God-modeled love, for "becoming one" with another. Or didn't you realize that your body is a sacred place, the place of the Holy Spirit? Don't you see that you can't live however you please, squandering what God paid such a high price for? The physical part of you is not some piece of property belonging to the spiritual part of you. God owns the whole works. So let people see God in and through your body.

(1 COR. 6:16–20, MSG)

Allow the truth of these words to realign your ideas about your sexuality.

_____

_____

_____

_____

Dear God,

_____

_____

_____

_____

DAY 3

But among you there must not be even a hint of sexual immorality,
or of any kind of impurity, or of greed, because these are improper
for God's holy people. Nor should there be obscenity, foolish talk or
coarse joking, which are out of place, but rather thanksgiving.

(EPH. 5:3–4)

After reading this verse, sit quietly in God's presence and allow the
Holy Spirit to reveal any inappropriate words or behaviors that are a
part of your life.

_____

_____

_____

_____

_____

Dear God,

_____

_____

_____

_____

_____

_____

DAY 4

Above all else, guard your heart,
for everything you do flows from it.
Keep your mouth free of perversity;
keep corrupt talk far from your lips.
Let your eyes look straight ahead;
fix your gaze directly before you.
Give careful thought to the paths for your feet
and be steadfast in all your ways.
Do not turn to the right or the left;
keep your foot from evil.

(PROV. 4:23–27)

Honestly consider the thoughts of your heart. Notice the progress in Proverbs 4, from the heart, to the mouth, to the eyes, to the steps. Allow the Holy Spirit to point out any unhealthy *thoughts* that could lead you down an undesirable path.

_____

_____

_____

_____

Dear God,

_____

_____

_____

_____

DAY 5

It is God's will that your honorable lives should silence those ignorant people who make foolish accusations against you. For you are free, yet you are God's slaves, so don't use your freedom as an excuse to do evil. Respect everyone, and love your Christian brothers and sisters. Fear God, and respect the king.

(1 PET. 2:15–17, NLT)

Consider the ways your respect (or lack of respect) for others displays what is in your heart.

_____

_____

_____

_____

_____

_____

_____

Dear God,

_____

_____

_____

_____

_____

_____

PERSONAL REFLECTION QUESTIONS

Have you ever been sexually exploited or abused? Have you been completely honest with God about how you feel? Is there anything you still need to tell Him about it?

If you are still hurting, allow God's love and grace to wash over every part of the pain. It can be healing to write out the emotions you are feeling. (If you are discouraged and feel that healing is a distant dream, don't hesitate to seek professional help.)

If you have committed sexual sin, read 1 Corinthians 6:16–20 to understand the effects of it in your life. Read John 8:3–11 to understand how Jesus would respond if you were standing in front of Him. Then read Psalm 51 to help you express your repentance and receive His forgiveness. Write out your own prayer.

Read through the cultural lies about sexuality (on page 135). Ask yourself if you have naively bought into any of those ideas. If so, re-read the corresponding Scripture passage revealing God's truth. Ask God to replace the cultural lies with His Word. (You might want to write the verse on a card to help you remember the truth.)

Are there things in your life such as books, movies, magazines, television programs, or conversations that cause you to be dissatisfied with your appearance, your spouse, or your sex life? Then consider the joy of living without dissatisfaction and decide to get rid of those things. Write out your decision and ask God to renew your perspective.

What boundaries do you have in place to help you guard your heart? Read through the ones listed on pages 139–141. Do you need to adopt any of these or reestablish ones you have decided for yourself?

_____

_____

_____

_____

_____

_____

_____

_____

_____

_____

_____

_____

_____

_____

_____

_____

_____

_____

_____

_____

Read through the warning signs that you are getting too close to a man other than your husband (if you are married) or a married man (if you are single). Are any of those signs revealing that you are too close to him? How can you correct the situation? Consider telling a close, mature Christian friend about the situation and ask her to help you make the right decisions.

_____

_____

_____

_____

_____

_____

_____

_____

_____

_____

_____

_____

_____

_____

_____

Do you ever find yourself being disrespectful to men? Consider what your responses disclose about your heart—are you placing unrealistic expectations on men? If so, consider how you can allow God to define you and meet your needs more effectively?

_____

_____

_____

_____

_____

_____

_____

_____

_____

_____

_____

_____

_____

_____

_____

_____

Honestly ask yourself if you flirt or dress inappropriately to attract men. Make a fresh commitment to respect yourself and men by making the necessary changes.

Write out a fresh commitment to sexual purity.

_____

_____

_____

_____

_____

_____

_____

_____

_____

_____

_____

_____

_____

_____

_____

NOTE: *As mothers and grandmothers, we need to share these truths with our children. It's important for them to know how to guard themselves against inaccurate views of sexuality and the danger of those who would want to expose and exploit them. Commit to educating your children in these areas.*

SCAN THIS CODE
WITH YOUR
SMARTPHONE
TO WATCH
A VIDEO
INTRODUCTION
TO THIS CHAPTER.

CHAPTER FIVE

Redeeming Relationships

Let the redeemed of the LORD tell their story.

PSALM 107:2

I had just arrived home from an out-of-town trip when my husband called to tell me that Chuck and Carolyn Myers' daughter-in-law and granddaughter had been murdered in Samson, Alabama, during a violent shooting rampage. Chuck and Carolyn are dear friends who attended our church at the time. Their oldest son, Josh, a deputy sheriff, moved to Alabama with his young family a few years ago. That day, his wife and two-year-old daughter were suddenly and brutally taken from his life.

What immense sorrow for our friends—losing a daughter-in-law and grandbaby in a senseless act of violence! How would they cope with the knowledge that their son, who puts his life on the line to protect others every day, had lost half of his family in a matter of seconds? How would their little grandbaby Ella and four-year-old Isaac make it without their mom and their sister, Corrine? How does a person even begin to process the emotions of such a loss?

I can't imagine all Chuck and Carolyn felt. And I don't want to make inaccurate speculations, but I think I know them well enough to know a few things. I'm quite sure they were so thankful for every moment they had spent with Andrea and Corrine. I'm sure they didn't regret anything they had sacrificed to show them love. I know the most important thing to them in that moment was to be with Josh and his other two children—to surround those they loved with as much support as it would take to journey through the sorrow.

OUR LOVE FOR GOD IS NOT JUST SEEN IN THE WAY WE TREAT OUR CLOSEST FAMILY MEMBERS AND FRIENDS, IT'S ALSO SEEN IN THE WAY WE TREAT STRANGERS.

I watched them rest completely in the arms of God. They wept, they grieved, and wept some more. But they faced every moment with a steady, unwavering faith—it was an inspiration to me. They believed God's grace would be sufficient for every moment, and He never disappointed them. Compelled by faith, Chuck and Caroline sacrificially moved to Alabama to support Josh and his little family. Their love prompted them to action, and they did whatever was necessary to support their son and grandchildren through an extremely difficult season of life.

Chuck and Caroline are now more aware of the important things in life—knowing and loving God, and loving and serving those He has given to us. Everything else is just "stuff." At the

end of it all, our jobs, our possessions, our positions, our plans
. . . *nothing* really matters except our relationship with God and
those He has given us to love.

Tragedy really does have a way of putting everything into
perspective and teaching us some extremely important lessons.
Andrea and Corrine's brief lives and sudden deaths taught me
to ask some important questions, questions that can help us
experience redeeming relationships:

- Do I live with the awareness that life is extremely
  fragile?
- Do I view every moment as a valuable gift from
  God?
- Do I strive to know and love God, so that when
  difficulties come into my life I am able to rest
  securely in Him?
- Do I take time to show the people in my life how
  much I love them?
- Do I give my best efforts, energy, and time to the
  most important things in life or am I consumed
  with temporal, less important things?

WHAT JESUS SAID ABOUT RELATIONSHIPS

Jesus tells us in Matthew 22:36–40 that nothing is more
important than loving God and loving others.

> "Teacher, which is the greatest commandment in the
> Law?" Jesus replied: "Love the LORD your God with
> all your heart and with all your soul and with all your

mind. This is the first and greatest commandment. And the second is like it: Love your neighbor as yourself. All the Law and the Prophets hang on these two commandments."

The command to "Love the Lord your God" is found twelve times in The New International Version of the Bible. And the phrase, "Love your neighbor" is found nine times. In addition to the "love your neighbor" command, more than forty New Testament verses contain the words "one another." These instructive passages tell us how to love each other. God really wants us to get this "loving" thing right.

We can say we love God, but if our treatment of others doesn't demonstrate love, we are just fooling ourselves (1 John 4:7–21). In Matthew 25:34–46 Jesus used the following story to explain how our love for God is seen in our treatment of others. One is a reflection of the other.

"Then the King will say to those on his right, 'Come, you who are blessed by my Father; take your inheritance, the kingdom prepared for you since the creation of the world. For I was hungry and you gave me something to eat, I was thirsty and you gave me something to drink, I was a stranger and you invited me in, I needed clothes and you clothed me, I was sick and you looked after me, I was in prison and you came to visit me.'

"Then the righteous will answer him, 'LORD, when did we see you hungry and feed you, or thirsty and give you something to drink? When did we see you a stranger and invite you in, or needing clothes and clothe you? When did we see you sick or in prison and go to visit you?'

"The King will reply, 'Truly I tell you, whatever you did for one of the least of these brothers and sisters of mine, you did for me.'

"Then he will say to those on his left, 'Depart from me, you who are cursed, into the eternal fire prepared for the devil and his angels. For I was hungry and you gave me nothing to eat, I was thirsty and you gave me nothing to drink, I was a stranger and you did not invite me in, I needed clothes and you did not clothe me, I was sick and in prison and you did not look after me.'

"They also will answer, 'LORD, when did we see you hungry or thirsty or a stranger or needing clothes or sick or in prison, and did not help you?'

"He will reply, 'Truly I tell you, whatever you did not do for one of the least of these, you did not do for me.'

"Then they will go away to eternal punishment, but the righteous to eternal life."

When we love God, love will be evident in the way we treat those closest to us. God's love was so evident in Chuck and Caroline's response to the tragedy their son faced. They quickly dropped everything to be with Josh and his children without any thought to their own comfort or desires. Then they willingly rearranged their entire lives to move close enough to help them with the challenge of facing everyday life without their wife and mother.

However, our love for God is not just seen in the way we treat our closest family members and friends, it's also seen in the way we treat strangers. Jesus' words in Matthew 25 challenge me to encounter every person as if I'm encountering Jesus—to realize that how I treat that individual is how I treat Him. My love for God is clearly seen in the way I interact with a restaurant server who doesn't get my order right . . . or the child who uses my yard for mud wrestling . . . or a friend who is caught in sin . . . or the homeless person who approaches me in a parking lot . . .

REDEMPTION

Since God *is* love, and we are continually being transformed into His image, His redeeming love should flow through our lives to everyone around us. In *every* personal encounter, we have the opportunity to reveal His grace. Here are a few ways we can bring redemption to others:

- We take full responsibility for ourselves and make it our goal to reflect the character of Christ in every personal encounter.
- We choose mercy over harsh judgments so God's grace can flow freely to others.
- We develop relationships with those who have more experience than we do, and then pay it forward by investing in others.
- We learn to handle conflict appropriately so our relationships become redemptive.

- We watch for opportunities to encourage others every day.

STRATEGIES TO REDEEM RELATIONSHIPS

1. Take Full Responsibility for Yourself

God created a perfect world where He enjoyed a close, intimate relationship with Adam and Eve. They also had an ideal relationship with one another. Genesis 2:25 says, "They were naked and knew no shame." This describes the open, honest relationship they enjoyed with each other. In the account of the fall (Gen. 3), we see also that God created humankind with a free will. He told Adam and Eve what was best for them, but it was up to them to make their own choices. (By the way, this is still true today. God doesn't control people's decisions, so why do we think we can?)

Adam and Eve chose to do what God had told them not to and as a result sin entered the world. Immediately the shame they felt gave way to the "blame game" (Gen. 3:8–13). Then in just a few short chapters we see dishonesty, jealousy, manipulation, and domineering control (even murder). All of these relational issues were the result of their fallen state (see Rom. 1:21–22).

Jesus is a perfect example of someone who took responsibility for Himself. His security was found in His relationship with His heavenly Father. He knew what He was on earth to do

IF WE FIND OURSELVES STRUGGLING IN OUR RELATIONSHIPS, THE PROBLEM MAY BE US.

REDEEMED! EMBRACING A TRANSFORMED LIFE

and never hesitated to do His Father's will. He responded with gracious confidence. He treated every individual with respect and spoke the truth in love. We never see Him being dishonest, defensive, jealous, bitter, resentful, harsh, or controlling.

If we find ourselves struggling in our relationships, the problem may be us. When I wrote the book for wives, *Secrets: Transforming Your Life and Marriage*, I had one of those "ah-ha" moments. I remember where I was sitting when this thought resounded in my heart, and I understood it fully—the way we treat others is a clear reflection of our own character. So many times we can be like Adam and Eve and blame our responses on the other person or the difficult circumstance we're facing. Thoughts like, *"That person makes me so angry, I can't help but . . . ,"* reveal a flaw in our own character.

> IT'S A WASTE OF TIME AND MENTAL ENERGY TO WISH THAT OTHER PEOPLE OR SITUATIONS WOULD CHANGE.

Dr. George O. Wood says people are a lot like water glasses—when you "bump" them, whatever is on the inside comes out. In every relationship we'll be "bumped." And the closer a relationship is, the more likely we are to have these collisions. So what do the "bumps" in our lives reveal about our hearts?

When we're jostled and we respond with jealousy, dishonesty, gossip, manipulation, pettiness, harsh words, critical attitudes, or defensive responses, we know it's time to do some self-examination. The difficult situation simply reveals what's already on the inside. The woman who has yielded control of her life to the Holy Spirit will display His fruit when she is bumped—she will respond with love, joy, peace, patience, kindness, goodness, faithfulness, gentleness, and self-control (Gal. 5:22–23, NLT).

We cannot be responsible for other people's responses or behaviors. Nor can we control many circumstances in our lives. It's a waste of time and mental energy to wish that other people or situations would change. We should use that time and energy to embrace God's grace and allow Him to redeem our thoughts, attitudes, and responses. The good news is, when we take responsibility for our behavior we can ask God for His help. Then He faithfully transforms our character to reflect His own. That's how we bring His redemption to all of our relationships.

2. Choose Mercy Over Harsh Judgment

Everyone needs mercy and forgiveness. Redemptive relationships will always be marked with God's grace. Max Lucado, one of my favorite wordsmiths, says—"We condemn a man for stumbling this morning, but we didn't see the blows he took yesterday. We judge a woman for the limp in her walk, but cannot see the tack in her shoe. . . . Not only are we ignorant about yesterday, we are ignorant about tomorrow. Dare we judge a book while chapters are yet unwritten? Should we pass a verdict on a painting while the artist still holds the brush? How can you dismiss a soul until God's work is complete?" [10]

What would judgment have looked like for Moses right after killing the Egyptian? Or David immediately after his affair, murder, and cover-up? Or the woman at the well before her encounter with Jesus? Or Peter the day after the crucifixion? The list is endless . . . "For if you refuse to act kindly, you can hardly expect to be treated kindly. Kind mercy wins over harsh judgment every time" (James 2:13, MSG).

3. Learn from Those with More Experience, then Pay It Forward

God lovingly places people in our lives who are more experienced than we are. We can learn important lessons from them. I'm so thankful we don't have to learn everything the hard way, through trial and error. (That's usually *really* painful!) We should intentionally seek out relationships with people who are more experienced than we are. Great mentors are individuals who have successfully walked a path we hope to walk—like a woman who lives and works with great integrity, a woman who enjoys a healthy marriage, a mom who has a great relationship with her adult children, or a woman who is navigating the next season of life with grace. We can learn important lessons by simply observing their lives and having meaningful conversations with them. If we listen and watch closely, we can avoid many mistakes.

Peggy Musgrove was one of those women in my own journey. When I was a young mom, she saw leadership abilities in me—abilities I never knew existed. She challenged me with opportunities that helped to stretch and develop my skills. Peggy was such a beautiful example of a woman in leadership that many times as a leader I ask myself, "What would Peggy do?"

Peggy told me how she asked the Lord for twelve women to influence. Following the pattern of Jesus, she wanted to *intentionally* invest in twelve people. I know I wouldn't be the person I am today without her loving influence. She challenges me to think about those I can invest significant time with— just living life and sharing God's truth in conversation and example. He directs our paths to intersect with others—some for a season, but others for a lifetime. (I want to encourage my daughter-in-law, Katie, and my granddaughter, Molly, as long as I have breath.)

We all benefit from having different types of relationships. Not only can we learn from people who are more experienced, we also gain different perspectives by hanging out with older and younger people. We become more compassionate when we have relationships with people who have special needs. And we can make a difference in a life when we connect with someone who doesn't yet know Christ.

EVERYONE NEEDS MERCY AND FORGIVENESS.

Will you make the same choice Peggy made and intentionally invest in others? Our time on earth is so brief, but when we choose to pour our energy and resources into those who are younger, our influence can live on for generations.

4. Handle Conflict with Grace

Everyone fails—even the most devoted Christ follower makes mistakes. If you're in relationships with people, at some point you'll be disappointed and even hurt. No question about it. We shouldn't be surprised by this—the Bible teaches we're all sinners and we all make mistakes. Author Dee Brestin states, "We need to mature to the point where we realize that while it is important to love and cherish our friends, our dependence should be in God alone—for only He is without sin, and only He will never let us down." [11]

Conflict is a part of our human existence. When we're hurt we have several options. The easiest and most natural response is to get angry, bitter, and hurt back. But this cycle leads to brokenness. We are also tempted to talk bad about the person who has offended us. This simply spreads the problem and resolves nothing. (It can also cause others to think negatively of us and not trust us to speak well of them.)

In *The Friendships of Women Workbook*, author Dee Brestin shares healthy strategies for dealing with conflict. She likens Christian women to roses—beautiful, yet not without thorns. [12] When we've been hurt by a friend we have two healthy options:

1. **Overlook the offense in love**—"Love covers a multitude of sins" (Prov. 10:12, 17:9; James 5:20; 1 Pet. 4:8). Consider how many offenses should be overlooked in love. Relationships can be full of unnecessary conflict over petty issues. Brestin says, "When a rose gardener is jabbed by a thorn, she realizes the rose had no personal animosity toward her but was simply born with thorns. We'd be wise to see people that way." [13] Pointing out every offense reveals our immaturity; we can learn not to take them personally. Proverbs 19:11 tells us, "A person's wisdom yields patience; it is to one's glory to overlook an offense."

2. **Confront in love**—"speaking the truth in love" (Eph. 4:15). The only motive to confront in times of conflict should be the desire to restore relationship and bring resolution. If the motive is to simply point out the offense or to hurt back, it's better to overlook the offense. The desire

for restoration should always be the motivation
for a confrontation. If someone has to win,
then someone has to lose, and this is extremely
unhealthy in any relationship. In Matthew
18, Jesus provides us with the right steps to
confront—first we speak to the person alone (it
should be kept between the people involved in
the conflict); if that doesn't bring resolution we
can include one or two wise people in the process.
The final step is to bring those in authority to the
conversation. We should take these steps to *restore*
our brother or sister in Christ.

Brestin also shares that we can be in a relationship with an
"alligator." The scriptural illustration she uses is that of King
Saul in his relationship with David—Saul was full of jealousy
and rage toward David. There is only one way to handle conflict
with an alligator:

1. **Forgiveness and flight.** "Do not make friends
   with a hot-tempered man, do not associate with
   one easily angered" (Prov. 22:24, NIV 1984).
   David showed us how to respond in such a
   situation. He never treated Saul with contempt or
   returned the vicious acts he received from Saul.
   He always responded with respect, but he didn't
   keep himself in the presence of one bent on doing
   him harm. He forgave and fled!

What great advice for dealing with conflict! Remember—
conflict with a friend doesn't mean that the relationship is

broken; it simply means that human beings are involved. We always have the choice to respond in a mature, healthy way. We can simply overlook the offense in love; confront in love to restore relationship; or, when dealing with an "alligator," we can forgive and flee while treating the "alligator" with respect.

5. Look for Ways to Encourage Others

When our son Tyler was thirteen years old he had major surgery on his right leg. It was the second surgery in a short time to correct the effects of dysplasia. He is now twenty-eight years old, and he still has the eight-inch plate and five screws in his leg. Even though it was more than a decade ago, I clearly remember the night before his surgery.

I walked past his room and heard quiet sobs. I knocked on the door and asked if I could come in. Tyler's shaky voice said, "Sure." He quickly wiped the tears streaming down his face as I walked into his room. I sat down on the side of his bed, looked into his face, and asked if I could do anything to help. Since this wasn't Tyler's first surgery, he knew exactly what he was facing in the coming days, so I wasn't surprised by the tears.

Tyler said, "Mom, I've just been praying and I know God can heal me—I could walk in the hospital tomorrow and they could see perfect bones with no reason to do the operation. But, I feel in my heart that I'll have the surgery and there's a reason for me to be in the hospital. Let's keep our eyes open for what God wants us to do—maybe He wants us to witness to a doctor or a nurse."

I promised him that I would help him look for the opportunity God had planned for us while we were at KU

Medical Center in the coming days. Then I prayed for Tyler to get a good night's sleep and to experience God's peace no matter what the next day held. We also prayed for his surgeon and everyone we would come in contact with at the hospital. When I walked out of his room, I was the one who was weeping. I was so moved by

GOD DIRECTS OUR PATHS TO INTERSECT WITH OTHERS— SOME FOR A SEASON, BUT OTHERS FOR A LIFETIME.

his faith. Tyler knew God's power to heal, but he also trusted His love enough to walk through the difficult place looking for a way to share God's love.

Tyler's surgery went well, but the first few days of recovery were extremely painful. They cut a wedge out of his femur to straighten the bone and attached an eight-inch plate to hold it in place. In spite of the pain, Tyler was emotionally strong and at peace. Even in the excruciating moments of physical therapy, tears made their way to the surface, but he always kept his composure.

Jessie, Tyler's roommate, wasn't having the same experience. For some reason, Jessie was in the hospital alone—there were no adults present to help him deal with the pain, get to the bathroom, or call for the nurse. Since either Mike or I were constantly with Tyler, we did what we could to help Jessie. One night Jessie was having an extremely difficult time. Tyler asked us to pull back the curtain separating the two beds so he could talk to him. I'll never forget how Tyler encouraged his roommate.

"Jessie, do you see how good I'm doing? I know it is because I have people praying for me. God is helping me to get through this. Do you have anyone praying for you?" Jessie made a point to tell us that that he didn't have anyone with him, or anyone praying for him. Tyler asked if he could pray for him. His prayer was simple, but powerful. Jessie calmed down and went to sleep for the first time since he was out of surgery. Later that night, when all was quiet in our room Tyler looked over at me and said, "Mom, we are here for Jessie."

CONFLICT WITH A FRIEND DOESN'T MEAN THAT THE RELATIONSHIP IS BROKEN; IT SIMPLY MEANS THAT HUMAN BEINGS ARE INVOLVED.

That night in the hospital, I was overwhelmed with God's love. He loved Jessie so much and He knew that he would face this difficult time in his life without the love and support of his family. So He sent our family to be His physical hands and to share words of comfort and peace.

Friends, we can look for ways to encourage others no matter what we face. Then the joy of serving someone else will quietly displace the sting of our own struggle.

CONCLUSION

When we look closely at the life of Christ, we see that He invested in individuals with brief impact moments—like His conversation with the woman at the well or the dinner He ate with sinners at Matthew's house. Let's not miss those important, God-planned opportunities. He may want to reveal Himself to someone through a simple conversation or a random act of kindness that He has planned for us today.

Other times God strategically places people in our lives for a season so we can consistently demonstrate His love to them. What a privilege to be His representative to people who need to know how much He wants to have a relationship with them. Whether it's a momentary encouragement or an ongoing relationship, let's look for every appointment He sets up.

Recently I have been challenged through various Facebook posts, blogs, and conversations with statements such as:

- Treat others *better* than you wish to be treated.
- Live to serve, not to be noticed.
- Consider giving up something you want for something someone else needs.
- Do for one what you wish you could do for many.
- Compassion is a lifestyle, not an event.

Jesus makes a similar challenge in John 13:34, "A new command I give you: Love one another. As I have loved you, so you must love one another." When we look closely at the life of Christ we can be overwhelmed with the idea of loving like He did. But what if we simply take it one day at a time and choose to love like He does *today?*

Every time we encounter another person we have an opportunity to love. It's encouraging to understand that love is an action, not simply a *feeling.* We may not be able to choose our feelings, but since love is an action, we can always *choose* to love.

In the "one another" passages of the New Testament we receive some practical advice for loving others. (All emphasis here is mine.)

- Be devoted to *one another* (Rom. 12:10).
- Encourage *one another* (2 Cor. 13:11; 1 Thess. 5:11; Heb. 3:13).

- Serve *one another* (Gal. 5:13).
- Be kind and compassionate to *one another* (Eph. 4:32).
- Forgive *one another* (Col. 3:13).
- Offer hospitality to *one another* (1 Pet. 4:9).

(You can find an entire list of "one another" verses in Appendix B.)

What if we spent an entire day focusing on the people we come in contact with and asking ourselves what we could do for them? *Do they need our attention or a few minutes of our time? How could we encourage them? Is there some way we could serve them? How could we offer them grace and forgiveness? What would be the kindest thing we could do for them?*

The story of our lives is told through our relationships—may they tell a beautiful, redemptive story!

Let the redeemed of the Lord tell their story.

PSALM 107:2

GROUP DISCUSSION

1. Tragedy has a way of helping us reprioritize our lives. How has a sudden loss challenged you to examine your priorities?

_____

_____

_____

_____

_____

_____

2. Understanding that the greatest commandment is to love God and others, how should we respond to Jesus' story in Matthew 25:24–36?

_____

_____

_____

_____

_____

_____

_____

3. I said that the way we treat others is a clear reflection of our character. What did Christ's treatment of people reveal about His character?

_____

_____

_____

_____

_____

_____

_____

4. If people are like water glasses—when they are "bumped" what is on the inside comes out—what should we do if we find we respond poorly with every little "jostle"?

_____

_____

_____

_____

_____

_____

_____

5. Why can we be more consumed with wanting to change others than looking honestly at ourselves?

_____

_____

_____

_____

_____

_____

_____

6. How can a woman who is genuinely filled with the Holy Spirit bring redemption to others?

_____

_____

_____

_____

_____

_____

_____

_____

7. Max Lucado says, "Dare we judge a book while chapters are yet unwritten? . . . How can you dismiss a soul until God's work is complete?" Discuss the ways mercy wins over harsh judgments.

_____

_____

_____

_____

_____

_____

_____

8. Discuss the value of having a variety of relationships. What can we learn from people who are more experienced or younger than we are?

_____

_____

_____

_____

_____

_____

_____

9. Read through the insights from Dee Brestin on handling conflict. What are the benefits of overlooking offenses? Confronting in love? And forgiving and fleeing?

_____

_____

_____

_____

_____

_____

_____

_____

10. Describe a time when you felt God encouraged you through someone—it could be a close friend, family member, or even a complete stranger.

_____

_____

_____

_____

_____

_____

_____

DAILY READING, MEDITATION, & PRAYER

Chapter Five: Redeeming Relationships

God works in our hearts as we read and meditate on His Word. Over the next five days, spend a few minutes every day allowing the truths you've discovered in chapter five to soak into your soul.

DAY 1

So I say, walk by the Spirit, and you will not gratify the desires of the flesh. For the flesh desires what is contrary to the Spirit, and the Spirit what is contrary to the flesh. They are in conflict with each other, so that you are not to do whatever you want. But if you are led by the Spirit, you are not under the law. The acts of the flesh are obvious: sexual immorality, impurity and debauchery; idolatry and witchcraft; hatred, discord, jealousy, fits of rage, selfish ambition, dissensions, factions and envy; drunkenness, orgies, and the like. I warn you, as I did before, that those who live like this will not inherit the kingdom of God. But the fruit of the Spirit is love, joy, peace, forbearance, kindness, goodness, faithfulness, gentleness and self-control. Against such things there is no law. Those who belong to Christ Jesus have crucified the flesh with its passions and desires. Since we live by the Spirit, let us keep in step with the Spirit.

(GAL. 5:16–25)

Consider your responses when you are "bumped" by others. Allow the Lord to show you where He wants to fill you and lead you.

_____

_____

_____

_____

_____

_____

_____

_____

Dear God,

_____

_____

_____

_____

_____

_____

_____

_____

DAY 2

Therefore let us stop passing judgment on one another.
Instead, make up your mind not to put any stumbling
block or obstacle in the way of a brother or sister.
(ROM. 14:13)

Allow the Lord to show you where you have a critical, judgmental spirit.

_____

_____

_____

_____

_____

_____

_____

Dear God,

_____

_____

_____

_____

_____

_____

_____

DAY 3

We know what real love is because Jesus gave up his life for us So we also ought to give up our lives for our brothers and sisters. If someone has enough money to live well and sees a brother or sister in need but shows no compassion—how can God's love be in that person? Dear children, let's not merely say that we love each other; let us show the truth by our actions.

(1 JOHN 3:16–18, NLT)

Consider how your love and treatment of people reflects your love of God.

_____

_____

_____

_____

_____

_____

_____

Dear God,

_____

_____

_____

_____

_____

_____

DAY 4

Finally, brothers and sisters, rejoice! Strive for full restoration,
encourage one another, be of one mind, live in peace. And
the God of love and peace will be with you.

(2 COR. 13:11)

Consider the ways you resolve conflict, and allow the Lord to show
you what brings restoration and peace.

_____

_____

_____

_____

_____

_____

_____

Dear God,

_____

_____

_____

_____

_____

_____

DAY 5

Don't look out only for your own interests,
but take an interest in others, too.

(PHIL. 2:4, NLT)

Spend some time repenting for the times you have simply looked out for yourself.

_____

_____

_____

_____

_____

_____

_____

Dear God,

_____

_____

_____

_____

_____

_____

_____

PERSONAL REFLECTION QUESTIONS

Ask yourself these questions:

Do I live with the awareness that life is extremely fragile?

_____

_____

_____

Do I view every moment as a valuable gift from God?

_____

_____

_____

Do I strive to know and love God, so when difficulties come into my life I am able to rest securely in Him?

_____

_____

_____

Do I take time to show the people in my life how much I love them?

_____

_____

Are my best efforts, energy, and time given to the most important things in life, or am I consumed with temporal, less important things?

_____

_____

_____

_____

_____

_____

_____

_____

_____

_____

_____

_____

_____

_____

_____

_____

What does the way you treat your family members say about your love for God?

_____

_____

_____

_____

_____

_____

_____

_____

_____

_____

_____

_____

_____

_____

_____

_____

_____

_____

_____

Read Matthew 25:34–36. Do you treat strangers like you would treat Jesus?

_____

_____

_____

_____

_____

_____

_____

_____

_____

_____

_____

_____

_____

_____

_____

_____

_____

_____

_____

When you are "bumped" by people or circumstances, what do your responses reveal about what is in your heart? (If your responses are not healthy, take time to repent and ask God to help you work on that part of your character.)

Do you tend to blame others or your circumstances for your behavior, or do you own all of your thoughts, attitudes, and behaviors?

_____

_____

_____

_____

_____

_____

_____

_____

_____

_____

_____

_____

_____

_____

_____

_____

_____

_____

_____

Are you quick to make judgments of others or do you consistently show mercy? How can you become more merciful?

_____

_____

_____

_____

_____

_____

_____

_____

_____

_____

_____

_____

_____

_____

_____

_____

_____

_____

_____

Do you have a variety of relationships in your life? Do you have any meaningful relationships with people who are more experienced? Less experienced? Someone who needs to experience God's love? How can you be more intentional about forming (or maintaining) those relationships?

Read through the section on handling conflict with grace. How can you handle conflicts more effectively?

_____

_____

_____

_____

_____

_____

_____

_____

_____

_____

_____

_____

_____

_____

_____

_____

_____

Read through all of the "one another" passages in Appendix B and choose three ways to love others this week.

_____

_____

_____

_____

_____

_____

_____

_____

_____

_____

_____

_____

_____

_____

_____

_____

_____

_____

_____

_____

_____

Think about the person you love the most. How would you like that person to describe the relationship he or she has with you? What (if any) changes should you make to that relationship?

_____

_____

_____

_____

_____

_____

_____

_____

_____

_____

_____

_____

_____

_____

_____

_____

_____

_____

_____

SCAN THIS CODE
WITH YOUR
SMARTPHONE
TO WATCH
A VIDEO
INTRODUCTION
TO THIS CHAPTER.

CHAPTER SIX

Redeeming the Time

See then that you walk circumspectly, not as fools but as wise,
redeeming the time, because the days are evil.
Therefore do not be unwise, but understand what the will of the LORD is.

EPHESIANS 5:15–17, NKJV

L ate one night, 35,000 feet above the Atlantic Ocean, I was challenged by a statement I'd written in my journal, "There is always time to do the will of God." I have difficulty sleeping on overseas flights, so I decided to spend the quiet moments reading and reflecting. I remember hearing the sound of the jet engines, looking out the window at the stars above and the vast waters below, and questioning myself, "If I honestly believe there is always enough time to do the will of God, then why do I feel so stressed, wishing for more hours in a day?"

My husband and I were leading a missions team of twenty-seven people from our church in Wichita, Kansas, to Ireland. While the plane was dark and everyone was sleeping (or at least trying to sleep), I pondered that thought-provoking statement—"There is always time to do the will of God" and all of its implications for the busyness and anxiety I felt.

We landed in Dublin and a wonderful Irish couple and a kind driver greeted us. They brought a small bus and two cars to transport our team to the Bible college where we would spend the next seven days. We piled into the vehicles and headed to one of the most beautiful spots on the earth—Carrig Eden in Greystones, Ireland, which sits on the stunning, rugged coastline. Needless to say, the sites of Ireland crowded out the thoughts from my devotional time on the plane. I was delightfully overwhelmed by cars driving on the left side of narrow roads, thatched roofed houses with brightly colored doors, and sheep filling the greenest hills I had ever seen.

GOD MADE PLENTY OF TIME FOR US TO DO HIS WILL.

Once we arrived at the Bible college, the students won our hearts, and we began our work. The Irish people are extremely relational; they enjoy taking time for "tea" and lingering over meals. I found the slower pace of life in Ireland refreshing. But it was a challenge for a few of our team members. My husband, Mike, went to a nearby hardware store and had to wait twenty minutes to make his purchase. The store owners heard him come in, but they told him from the back room that they were enjoying their "cuppa tea." He simply had to stand and wait for them to finish before he could buy what he needed. (The thought of him standing there waiting while they drank their tea still makes me smile.) We soon realized that Ireland was challenging our fast-paced way of life.

One evening, after a full day's work and a delicious, home-cooked Irish meal, several of us took a walk along the shore. We met a kind, elderly gentleman who had lived in the area all his life. He greeted us warmly and initiated a conversation. His Irish accent captivated us, and we found his knowledge of Ireland so enlightening that we talked to him late into the evening. I don't remember much about what he told us, but I do remember his love for Ireland and how he made us feel— welcomed and valuable enough to give us his time. After an overview of Irish history and a few folk stories, we thanked him for taking so much time with us. I will never forget his response, "Oh, that's alright . . . because when God made time, He made plenty of it."

I remember thinking, *Wow, we aren't in Kansas anymore . . .* I had *never* heard that statement before. *Really—God made plenty of time?* In my fast-paced, American way of living, I always seem to long for more hours in the day, more days in the week, and more months in the year! (It was a bit ironic that on our sightseeing day we discovered that the phrase, "When God made time, He made plenty of it," is a common Irish saying. It's printed on clocks, wall plaques, and other souvenirs.)

Later in the week, Mike asked each of us to share with the group what God had done in our hearts through our time in Ireland. I was able to talk about God's clear challenge to me: He is the maker of time, and I need to allow Him to be the author of *my* time. I was beginning to believe that if I allowed Him to plan my day, I would achieve all He desired for me to accomplish with less stress. I told the group I was determined to reevaluate how I spent my time.

That week in Ireland challenged me to ask myself some important questions when I start to feel overwhelmed. *What am I doing that God doesn't want or need me to do? Am I neglecting the things that are important to Him? Am I allowing Him to lead my days, or am I letting the expectations of others influence how I spend my time? Am I taking too much time for things that are less important and temporal?* I hope I never forget the words of the old Irish saying, "When God made time, He made plenty of it," and the way He challenged my heart when a kind Irishman shared it with us.

TWO DAYS ON MY CALENDAR

Since that missions trip, God continues to challenge the way I view time. Recently I heard a quote by Martin Luther, "There are only two days on my calendar—this day and that day!" *This day* is today, and *that day* is the day we will stand before God in eternity. I've come to understand that this moment, the one I'm currently living, is the only moment in time I can experience His presence. It's the only time I can be obedient, extend His grace, or demonstrate His love. Today is what I have, and while there is no promise of tomorrow, there is the promise of the day I will stand in His presence.

It's a simple idea, but it has changed the way I approach every day. As I reflected on Luther's statement, I soon realized I wasn't living fully in the moment. I was spending too many days consumed with the past or worried about the future, and I was missing out on the

WE'RE SHAPED BY MOMENTARY DECISIONS MORE THAN WE REALIZE— EVEN THE SMALL, SEEMINGLY INSIGNIFICANT ONES.

opportunities of each day. I also discovered that I wasn't allowing the reality of eternity to impact the way I was living today.

REDEMPTION

The apostle Paul challenges us to "redeem the time," to be wise, and to understand God's will for our lives (Eph. 5:15–17). This can be quite a challenge with so many things clamoring for our attention and time. Consider the ideas I shared with you earlier: God made plenty of time for us to do His will, and we can live today with the promise that we will stand in His presence. Understanding these realities and making the following wise choices will help us to discover God's will for our lives and make the most of our time:

- Remember the importance of each moment.
- Seize the opportunities of each day.
- Embrace the realities of our current season.
- Look expectantly toward eternity.

STRATEGIES TO REDEEM THE TIME

1. Remember the Importance of the Moment

We can easily overlook the significance of the moment; even fail to see the connection between a momentary decision and a lasting consequence. I heard Pastor John Cremeans once say, "I am the sum total of all of my decisions." What an important truth to remember!

The "all" in that sentence includes *every* decision. Initially, we may think life-altering choices are the most important ones—like who we marry or what job we take. No one would argue that those are incredibly important decisions, but I believe the small, everyday choices have the potential to make the greatest impact. We're shaped by momentary decisions more than we realize—even the small, seemingly insignificant ones.

I can just imagine what you might be thinking right now. *Really, Kerry? The choice to give my best to a work assignment is as important as deciding what job I will take?* Let me explain—over time, the moment-by-moment choices we make define our character. Proverbs 20:11 (NIV 1984) tells us, "Even a child is known by his actions." Who we are and what we become happens one moment at a time, one decision at a time. Then, those momentary choices shape how we make the life-changing ones and determine our ability to sustain the right things in the long-term.

We face seemingly insignificant decisions all day long. Simple things like—*Should I eat the cheeseburger and fries or the salad? Do I feel like going to church this morning or can I sleep in? Do I really have to forgive that person or can I get even? Do I have to be kind or can I go with how I feel and be offensive?* If we think these decisions are insignificant, we'll believe the choices don't matter—cheeseburger or salad, go to church or stay home, hold a grudge or let it go, be kind or rude.

In his book *Crazy Love*, Francis Chan quotes Annie Dillard, "How we live our days is . . . how we live our lives."[14] I love the truth of that simple statement—our moment-by-moment choices become our lives. I don't think any woman would say, "I hope to become physically unhealthy, spiritually dead, emotionally numb, and relationally broken." But her *momentary* decisions are screaming exactly that.

We can redeem the time by remembering that the simple decisions we make *every moment* are setting a course for our future. In fact, the quality of our lives is determined by the *momentary* choices we make. So let's choose well!

2. Seize the Opportunities of the Day

I'm embarrassed to admit that I've spent many days longing for a different one—longing for Friday afternoon on Monday morning; longing for the day my newborn would sleep through the night when I was up rocking him at 2:00 a.m.; longing for the warmth of spring in the middle of a snow storm. If we aren't careful, our longings can cause us to completely miss *today!*

THE SIMPLE DECISIONS WE MAKE *EVERY MOMENT* ARE SETTINC A COURSE FOR OUR FUTURE.

God's Word challenges us to discover God's will. But, do you ever find yourself so consumed with what God has for your *future* that you lose sight of today? Or are you tempted to long for the "good ole days" of the past, when you felt your life was closer to God's plan? When we live focused on the future, we can allow restlessness and anxiety to rob us of the opportunities and pleasures of today. If we spend our time wishing for the past, we can become discouraged and discontent with today.

Recently, this thought occurred to me—*we can only be where we are.* (I know, what a profound thought, right?) But sometimes we fail to be where we are. Our thoughts are racing on about all of the things we have to do. Or we're worried and upset about what tomorrow may hold. Sometimes we're so distracted by what's going on in other people's lives that we completely neglect our own. Our smartphones add a whole new dimension to this reality. We can be in a meeting that demands our participation, but instead of really being there, we're answering an unrelated e-mail, checking a friend's Facebook status, looking at the most recent pins on Pinterest, or managing our stocks without ever leaving the meeting table. But what if we lived fully in the day and gave our best attention to what the day offered? I believe we would experience God's goodness on a whole new level. Our anxiety would be replaced with peace. And we would be more productive and content.

Solomon encourages us with these words:

There is a time for everything,
and a season for every activity under the heavens:
a time to be born and a time to die,
a time to plant and a time to uproot,
a time to kill and a time to heal,
a time to tear down and a time to build,
a time to weep and a time to laugh,
a time to mourn and a time to dance,
a time to scatter stones and a time to gather them,
a time to embrace and a time to refrain
from embracing,
a time to search and a time to give up,
a time to keep and a time to throw away,
a time to tear and a time to mend,

a time to be silent and a time to speak,
a time to love and a time to hate,
a time for war and a time for peace.
(ECCL. 3:1–8)

What if we really lived today the way God created it to be lived? If it's a day to rest, then rest completely, not distractedly. If it's a day to plan, then focus on the task at hand and plan! If it's a day to spend with your family, relish every moment by lavishing your love on them! If it's a day to celebrate, enjoy each moment and praise God for His goodness! If it's a time to mourn, experience the pain but know you will be comforted! If it's a day to serve, serve as if you were serving Jesus! (I think you get the point.)

I really want you to know that you can experience God's blessings when you embrace the unique opportunities of each new day. Here are a few of those benefits:

- Discovering God's will is a day-by-day process.
  We can be obedient today and discover His
  will for this day. Some people completely miss
  God's will for their lives because they think it's
  out there, somewhere in the future. But God
  wants to meet us right where we are and lead
  us moment by moment, step by step. He rarely
  gives us a long-range calendar filled with future
  appointments. But He will lead us today! And
  the awesome thing is, we will find His will for our
  future as we are obedient in His will today.

- We can remember God's goodness throughout our lives, but today we can *experience* His love in a fresh new way. Every good thing in our lives is a gift from Him; let's not miss the blessings of this day. We can watch for the continual love notes He sends our way—the sunrise, a meal we enjoy with friends, the belly laugh of a toddler, or the even the clothes we wear. Embracing each day helps us to live continually in His love.

- Seizing the day gives us the opportunity to experience God's presence. Right now we can enjoy the peace His presence brings into our lives. A peace that isn't dependent upon our circumstances, it's a calm that transcends what is going on around us. But we can only experience it here and now.

- We can love the people God places in our paths *today*. We shouldn't wait for "someday" to demonstrate our love. Those same people who are here today may not be there tomorrow. Seize the day to love well!

- We can trust God fully in the moment of today—believing His grace is more than sufficient for every need we may face. Just as He provided manna for the Israelites on their journey through the wilderness, He will provide exactly what we need today.

- Since God's mercies are new every morning, we don't have to worry about tomorrow, because when we get there, He will be there too.

So don't give so much thought to *some* day—trust God completely with *this* day. And you can experience the reality of Psalm 16:11 (NIV 1984), "You have made known to me the path of life, you will fill me with joy in your presence, with eternal pleasures at your right hand."

3. Embrace the Realities of Your Current Season

It's easy to embrace a season when we experience growth and obvious blessings. But if your life is anything like mine, seasons can change quickly, and we can find ourselves in a difficult, challenging place overnight. How do we embrace those difficult seasons for all they have to offer without becoming frustrated with the challenges they bring?

How easily we can find ourselves grumbling when things get hard. I know I have! Several years ago, Mike and I were serving as lead pastors and I was adjusting to a new responsibility—serving as an independent contractor for our denomination's national office. And

YOU CAN EXPERIENCE GOD'S BLESSINGS WHEN YOU EMBRACE THE UNIQUE OPPORTUNITIES OF EACH NEW DAY.

to be completely honest, a few months into the new job I began to feel overwhelmed. That's when the internal complaining began: *"How am I supposed to give 100 percent to the national office and 100 percent to our local congregation? I don't like being away from my husband, family, and church family one week a month."* Grumble, grumble, grumble went the self-focused melody of my heart.

In spite of a negative attitude, the Lord was so kind to use the retreat message of a dear friend Joanna Weaver (author of *Having a Mary Heart in a Martha World)* to challenge me with an incredible truth: *Don't despise the Lord's discipline, embrace it.* Immediately my mind went to Hebrews 12:7 (NIV 1984) where we are encouraged to "endure hardship as discipline." Verse 11 tells us that "no discipline seems pleasant at the time, but painful. Later on, however, it produces a harvest of righteousness and peace for those who have been trained by it."

When I was a young mother, the Lord challenged me with the idea of enduring hardship as discipline. This was a completely foreign idea to me. Growing up I had always viewed hardship, as . . . well . . . hard! It was something I simply wanted to pray away; I definitely did not want to endure it. The first time I considered this idea, I wanted to rationalize which hardships I would have to view as discipline. *I should only be disciplined by those difficulties I create, right? Surely, I don't have to be disciplined by other people's mistakes or circumstances beyond my control!* But the Lord helped me to see that no matter what the challenge was or who had caused it, He wanted me to endure it as discipline.

> WE DON'T HAVE TO WORRY ABOUT TOMORROW, BECAUSE WHEN WE GET THERE, HE WILL BE THERE TOO.

Challenging seasons come to us in many forms—illness, loss, strife in relationships, and even new "opportunities." Not only do they come in different forms, they can come from a variety of sources. We may want to blame every trial on Satan—and some of them are a direct attack from him. But the truth is, some of our difficulties are consequences of our own bad choices, others are a result of someone else's mistakes, and others are simply a by-product of life (like aging and providing for our families). And we are challenged when God leads us through a season of pruning, a painful time when He removes something from our lives to help us grow stronger. We may even experience difficulty when God stretches us by bringing us an exciting, new responsibility.

No matter what kind of difficult season we encounter or who we think caused it, we have two choices every time we walk through a challenge:

1. Despise the circumstance with whining, complaining, and grumbling, and pray God will make it go away.
2. Trust God enough to walk submissively as He leads us through the situation and believe He will make all things right in His timing.

The first choice is the most natural response; it's easy to grumble our way through a difficulty. We may even feel justified in our bad attitudes. But whining never made anything better. In fact, we may think a complaining spirit is harmless, but if it's left unchecked it always leads to bitterness. The writer of Hebrews warns us to, "watch out that no poisonous root of bitterness grows up to trouble you, corrupting many" (12:15, NLT). Bitterness will not only hurt our lives, it will harm those closest to us.

On the other hand, when we embrace hardship, this leads to maturity and produces good things in our lives. Here are a few ideas to help us embrace difficult seasons as God's discipline:

1. Believe God will work *all* things for our good.

2. Remember that when we seek Him, we will find Him. Run *to* Him, not *away* from Him in the midst of difficulty.
3. Keep our eyes on Him, not our circumstances; one builds faith, the other despair.
4. Live for God's eternal purposes not self-focused, temporal ones.
5. Believe that where He leads us, He will provide strength, peace, wisdom, or whatever is needed.
6. Wait for Him to deliver us.
7. Trust His love, even when nothing makes sense!

It's amazing what happens when we simply change our focus from self-centered pity to God-focused humility and submission—there we find righteousness and peace. James, Jesus' brother, encourages us to embrace the difficult seasons with these words:

> Consider it pure joy, my brothers, whenever you face trials of many kinds, because you know that the testing of your faith develops perseverance. Perseverance must finish its work so that you may be mature and complete, not lacking anything.
> (JAMES 1:2-4, NIV 1984)

We don't have to experience great trials to find ourselves complaining. Some seasons aren't difficult; they're just mundane and monotonous. When life feels tedious, if we're not careful we become self-focused and our attitudes become negative. So how do we embrace the "boring" seasons of life?

I remember an afternoon in a particularly "blah" period. Nothing major was going on in my life. I felt bogged down by a humdrum routine and some ongoing frustrations with work. (I'm guessing you have been there, too.) As I sat in my home office, working and trying to fight off the grey cloud hanging over my head, it started to rain. I *really* love sunshine, and the rain just added to my heaviness.

A few minutes after it started to rain, something outside the window caught my eye. I turned my chair to see the movement and was instantly mesmerized. Our neighbor's twelve-year-old daughter was dancing in the rain. She was whirling and leaping with her face upward and her arms outstretched—soaking up every drop of rain possible. Her ballet moves were beautiful, but it was her innocence and uninhibited enjoyment of the rain that I found so compelling. Something in my heart longed to dance with her.

Earlier that morning I had read Psalm 16:11, "You will fill me with joy in your presence." I wondered if my focus on the current "grey season" was causing me to miss the opportunity to "dance in the rain." *Had I allowed this mundane season of life to overwhelm the best part of life—God's presence?* I was missing the opportunity to throw my arms open wide and embrace His presence. While my twelve-year-old neighbor simply danced in the rain, she inspired me to embrace God's presence in spite of the "rain"—to live faithfully for Him and grateful to Him even in the mundane moments of life. Pastor David Lindell said it perfectly in a recent sermon:

WHEN WE EMBRACE HARDSHIP, THIS LEADS TO MATURITY AND PRODUCES GOOD THINGS IN OUR LIVES.

"Extraordinary things can't happen without faithfulness in the mundane, ordinary moments."

So, what season are you in? Are you embracing it or despising it? One leads to life and the other to despair.

4. Look Expectantly Toward Eternity

We can easily distract a baby from an unwanted object by simply removing the item from her view. In her limited development, she thinks something doesn't exist if she can't see it. And while it doesn't take much growth for babies to start looking beyond their view for the hidden item, most of us never fully develop an awareness of things that are not readily perceived.

We're so limited by time and space that we often live without thought of eternity or the brevity of our earthly lives. But we have constant reminders along the way—a young person loses his life in a car accident, a mother dies of complications from a routine surgery, a husband dies from injuries sustained in a work-related mishap. Even when someone lives for ninety-plus years, one life is extremely brief in the light of human history. We're never ready to say good-bye to the people we love, no matter how old or sick they are. But everyone's life on earth will come to an end.

WE'RE SO LIMITED BY TIME AND SPACE THAT WE OFTEN LIVE WITHOUT THOUGHT OF ETERNITY.

Aren't you thankful that this life *isn't* all there is? Revelation 21:3–4 shares the amazing reality of eternity for those who are redeemed:

Now the dwelling of God is with men, and he will live with them. They will be his people, and God himself will be with them and be their God. He will wipe every tear from their eyes. There will be no more death or mourning or crying or pain.

With the reminders of life's brevity and the wonderful promises of heaven, how should we live? Are we like the baby— if something is out of sight it is out of mind? Or are we making the best momentary decisions, living fully in the day, embracing each season, all the while looking expectant y toward that day when we will stand in God's presence?

CONCLUSION

God gives us life and then grants us a limited number of days to experience His goodness on earth. I love to think about the ways He reveals Himself through creation. The changing seasons declare His faithfulness. His provision for wildlife proclaims His care. The vastness of our universe screams His majesty. The breath-taking beauty of nature displays His creativity. Night declares His rest, and each sunrise reminds us that His mercies are new every morning.

Every day we experience His presence in tangible ways. In the warmth of a sunset, we feel His embrace. In the taste of an apple, the smell of honeysuckle, or the refreshment of cool water we experience His goodness. In the affection of our family we glimpse His love. In the forgiveness of a friend we experience His mercy.

Not only do creation and our life experiences tell us about God, but His Word tells us that He loved us so much that He sent His Son to our world so we could know Him even better. Jesus showed us exactly what God is like. Then in the greatest act of love, Jesus willingly laid down His life for our sin (all of those things that harm us and separate us from our loving, righteous Creator.) Through His Word we can know Him and His plan of redemption.

This faithful, caring, majestic, creative, embracing, and good God wants us to experience all He has for us. Each day He gives us is a precious gift! Within the span of our lives He wants us to know Him, to love Him, and to reveal His love to those around us. And He longs for us to do the things He created us to do. May God help us to redeem the time He gives us here on earth!

The creation we see is only a glimpse of the magnificence of heaven. We are told that "no eye has seen, no ear has heard, no mind has conceived what God has prepared for those who love him" (1 Cor. 2:9, NIV 1984). The glimpse of heaven described in Revelation 21 is absolutely breathtaking: God's glory is radiant and nothing impure can enter. Jesus tells us in John 14:1–3, NLT:

> "Don't let your hearts be troubled. Trust in God, and trust also in me. There is more than enough room in my Father's home. If this were not so, would I have told you that I am going to prepare a place for you? When everything is ready, I will come and get you, so that you will always be with me where I am."

Since we can only experience the moment we are currently living, let's not lose sight of the significance of every decision we make. Are we choosing to live in light of God's presence—are we aware of Him right now? Are we experiencing the benefits of living fully in *this* day and giving ourselves completely to the responsibilities right in front of us? Do we trust His love enough to face whatever today may bring? Do we know how to embrace every season, refusing to despise the difficult places?

Don't grow weary, my friend, for someday soon we will stand in God's presence completely whole and will experience a joy we can only imagine—the joy of the redeemed!

GROUP DISCUSSION

1. Read Ephesians 5:15–17, then discuss the implications of the idea that there is always time to do the will of God.

_____

_____

_____

_____

_____

_____

_____

_____

2. Describe the importance of redeeming our time.

_____

_____

_____

_____

_____

_____

_____

3. What happens when we fail to see the significance of momentary decisions? How can we remember the importance of the moment?

_____

_____

_____

_____

_____

_____

_____

_____

4. What are some distractions that keep us from living fully today?

_____

_____

_____

_____

_____

_____

_____

_____

5. What does it mean to "seize the day"?

_____

_____

_____

_____

_____

_____

_____

_____

6. How do we benefit when we give our full attention to what is right in front of us?

_____

_____

_____

_____

_____

_____

_____

_____

7. Some things last for a season, not just a day. When we experience a difficult time, how can we guard our hearts from bitterness? (Read the thoughts on pages 223–224.)

_____

_____

_____

_____

_____

_____

_____

8. Describe what it would be like to embrace Martin Luther's philosophy, "There are only two days on my calendar, *this day* and *that day.*" How can we live *this day* in light of *that day?*

_____

_____

_____

_____

_____

_____

_____

DAILY READING, MEDITATION, & PRAYER

Chapter Six: Redeeming the Time

God works in our hearts as we read and meditate on His Word. Over the next five days, spend a few minutes every day allowing the truths you've discovered in chapter six to soak into your soul.

DAY 1

See then that you walk circumspectly, not as fools but as wise, redeeming the time, because the days are evil. Therefore do not be unwise, but understand what the will of the LORD is.

(EPH. 5:15–17, NKJV)

Consider how you use your time, and ask the Holy Spirit to show you areas you need to adjust.

_____

_____

_____

Dear God,

_____

_____

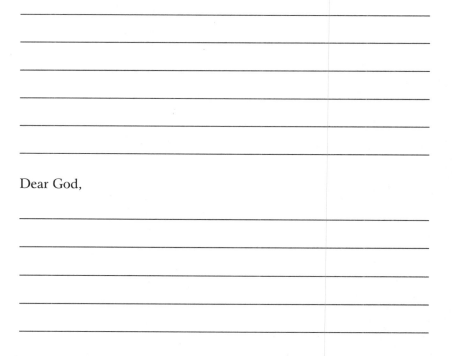

DAY 2

Today I have given you the choice between life and death, between blessings and curses. Now I call on heaven and earth to witness the choice you make. Oh, that you would choose life, so that you and your descendants might live! You can make this choice by loving the LORD your God, obeying him, and committing yourself firmly to him. This is the key to your life.
(DEUT. 30:19–20, NLT)

Allow the Lord to show you how your momentary decisions impact your life.

_____

_____

_____

_____

_____

_____

Dear God,

_____

_____

_____

_____

_____

_____

DAY 3

The faithful love of the LORD never ends!
His mercies never cease.
Great is his faithfulness;
his mercies begin afresh each morning.
I say to myself, "The LORD is my inheritance;
therefore, I will hope in him!"

(LAM. 3:22–24, NLT)

Ask the Lord to reveal to you the joy of living fully in the day.

_____

_____

_____

_____

_____

_____

Dear God,

_____

_____

_____

_____

_____

_____

DAY 4

Trust in the LORD *with all your heart;*
do not depend on your own understanding.
Seek his will in all you do,
and he will show you which path to take.
Don't be impressed with your own wisdom.
Instead, fear the LORD *and turn away from evil.*
Then you will have healing for your body
and strength for your bones.
Honor the LORD *with your wealth*
and with the best part of everything you produce.
Then he will fill your barns with grain,
and your vats will overflow with good wine.
My child, don't reject the LORD'S *discipline,*
and don't be upset when he corrects you.
For the LORD *corrects those he loves,*
just as a father corrects a child in whom he delights.

(PROV. 3:5–12, NLT)

Take some time today to rest in the knowledge that God is directing your paths—you don't have to figure everything out.

_____

_____

_____

_____

_____

_____

_____

_____

_____

Dear God,

_____

_____

_____

_____

_____

_____

_____

_____

_____

DAY 5

*Then I saw "a new heaven and a new earth," for the first heaven and
the first earth had passed away, and there was no longer any sea. I saw
the Holy City, the new Jerusalem, coming down out of heaven from God,
prepared as a bride beautifully dressed for her husband. And I heard a
loud voice from the throne saying, "Look! God's dwelling place is now
among the people, and he will dwell with them. They will be his people,
and God himself will be with them and be their God. 'He will wipe
every tear from their eyes. There will be no more death' or mourning
or crying or pain, for the old order of things has passed away."
He who was seated on the throne said, "I am making everything new!"
Then he said, "Write this down, for these words are trustworthy and true."
He said to me: "It is done. I am the Alpha and the Omega, the
Beginning and the End. To the thirsty I will give water without cost from
the spring of the water of life. Those who are victorious will inherit
all this, and I will be their God and they will be my children.*

(REV. 21:1–7)

Read this passage slowly and allow the reality of eternity to renew
your perspective.

Dear God,

PERSONAL REFLECTION QUESTIONS

Reflecting on your own life, do you feel "there is time to do the will of God?" Do you feel you *are* doing His will?

_____

_____

_____

_____

_____

_____

_____

_____

_____

_____

_____

_____

_____

_____

_____

_____

_____

_____

_____

What changes could you make to manage your time better?

_____

_____

_____

_____

_____

_____

_____

_____

_____

_____

_____

_____

_____

_____

_____

_____

_____

_____

_____

_____

Think about the statement, "I am the sum total of all my decisions."
What can you do to improve the everyday decisions you make?

_____

_____

_____

_____

_____

_____

_____

_____

_____

_____

_____

_____

_____

_____

_____

_____

_____

_____

_____

How can you embrace the day you are living? Think about the value of giving your best to this day—whatever it holds.

_____

_____

_____

_____

_____

_____

_____

_____

_____

_____

_____

_____

_____

_____

_____

_____

_____

_____

_____

What difficulties do you currently face? What is your attitude towards them? Are you embracing the current reality or grumbling against it? How can you view this time as discipline, learning and growing from what it can teach you?

_____

_____

_____

_____

_____

_____

_____

_____

_____

_____

_____

_____

_____

_____

_____

_____

_____

Read Revelation 21, perhaps in several different translations. Are you looking expectantly toward that day when you stand in God's presence? Describe how you might live differently if you kept eternity in your thoughts.

Reread the conclusion of this chapter and write your own commitment to redeeming your time.

ENDNOTES

1. http://www.merriam-webster.com/dictionary/redeem, accessed 8/23/12.

2. Brother Lawrence, *The Practice of the Presence of God* (Uhrichsville, OH: Barbour and Company, Inc., 1993), 37–38.

3. Andy Stanley, *The Principle of the Path* (Nashville, TN: Thomas Nelson, Inc., 2011), 44.

4. Joan Jacobs Brumberg, *The Body Project: An Intimate History of American Girls* (New York: Vintage, 1998).

5. Ruth Haley Barton, *Strengthening the Soul of Your Leadership: Seeking God in the Crucible of Ministry* (Downers Grove, IL: InterVarsity Press, 2008), 111–113.

6. Tom Holladay, *The Relationship Principles of Jesus* (Grand Rapids, MI: Zondervan, 2008), 320.

7. Special thanks to Andrea for her permission to include her post.

8. *New York Times*, http://www.nytimes.com/2011/12/15/health/nearly-1-in-5-women-in-us-survey-report-sexual-assault.html, accessed 9/1/12.

9. Jim P. Vigil, *Naked but Not Ashamed: A Theology of Marital Intimacy* (doctoral thesis). Trinity Evangelical Divinity School, 2007.

10. Max Lucado, *Grace for the Moment* (Nashville, TN: Thomas Nelson, Inc., 2000), 149.

11. Dee Brestin. *The Friendships of Women Workbook* (Wheaton, IL.: Victor Books, 1995), 174–178.

12. Ibid.

13. Ibid.

14. Francis Chan. *Crazy Love: Overwhelmed by a Relentless God* (Colorado Springs: David C. Cook, 2008), 163.

EPILOGUE

Remember—
Put your hope in the LORD,
for with the LORD is
unfailing love
and with him is full
redemption.
PSALM 130:7, NIV

And now . . .

May the LORD bless you
and protect you.
May the LORD smile on you
and be gracious to you.
May the LORD show you his favor
and give you his peace.
NUMBERS 6:24–26, NLT

APPENDIX A

THE "I AM" PASSAGES OF JESUS

John 6:35
Then Jesus declared, "*I am* the bread of life. Whoever comes to me will never go hungry, and whoever believes in me will never be thirsty."

John 6:51
"*I am* the living bread that came down from heaven. Whoever eats this bread will live forever. This bread is my flesh, which I will give for the life of the world."

John 8:12
When Jesus spoke again to the people, he said, "*I am* the light of the world. Whoever follows me will never walk in darkness, but will have the light of life."

John 8:23
But he continued, "You are from below; *I am* from above. You are of this world; *I am* not of this world."

John 8:58
"Very truly I tell you," Jesus answered, "before Abraham was born, *I am!*"

John 9:5
"While *I am* in the world, *I am* the light of the world."

John 10:9
"*I am* the gate; whoever enters through me will be saved. They will come in and go out, and find pasture."

John 10:11
"*I am* the good shepherd. The good shepherd lays down his life for the sheep."

John 10:14
"*I am* the good shepherd; I know my sheep and my sheep know me"

John 11:25
Jesus said to her, "*I am* the resurrection and the life. The one who believes in me will live, even though they die."

John 14:6
Jesus answered, "*I am* the way and the truth and the life. No one comes to the Father except through me."

John 14:11
"Believe me when I say that *I am* in the Father and the Father is in me; or at least believe on the evidence of the works themselves."

John 14:20
"On that day you will realize that *I am* in my Father, and you are in me, and *I am* in you."

John 14:28
"You heard me say, '*I am* going away and *I am* coming back to you.' If you loved me, you would be glad that *I am* going to the Father, for the Father is greater than I."

John 15:1
"*I am* the true vine, and my Father is the gardener."

John 15:5
"*I am* the vine; you are the branches. If you remain in me and I in you, you will bear much fruit; apart from me you can do nothing."

John 16:7
"But very truly I tell you, it is for your good that *I am* going away. Unless I go away, the Advocate will not come to you; but if I go, I will send him to you."

John 20:17
Jesus said, "Do not hold on to me, for I have not yet ascended to the Father. Go instead to my brothers and tell them, '*I am* ascending to my Father and your Father, to my God and your God.'"

John 20:21
Again Jesus said, "Peace be with you! As the Father has sent me, *I am* sending you."

Matthew 11:29
"Take my yoke upon you and learn from me, for *I am* gentle and humble in heart, and you will find rest for your souls."

Matthew 28:20
"Surely *I am* with you always, to the very end of the age."

Revelation 1:17
When I saw him, I fell at his feet as though dead. Then he placed his right hand on me and said: "Do not be afraid. *I am* the First and the Last."

Revelation 1:18
"*I am* the Living One; I was dead, and now look, *I am* alive for ever and ever! And I hold the keys of death and Hades."

Revelation 2:23
"*I am* he who searches hearts and minds, and I will repay each of you according to your deeds."

Revelation 3:11
"*I am* coming soon. Hold on to what you have, so that no one will take your crown."

Revelation 3:20
"Here *I am!* I stand at the door and knock. If anyone hears my voice and opens the door, I will come in and eat with that person, and they with me."

Revelation 21:5
He who was seated on the throne said, "*I am* making everything new!" Then he said, "Write this down, for these words are trustworthy and true."

Revelation 21:6
He said to me: "It is done. *I am* the Alpha and the Omega, the Beginning and the End. To the thirsty I will give water without cost from the spring of the water of life."

Revelation 22:7
"Look, *I am* coming soon! Blessed is the one who keeps the words of the prophecy written in this scroll."

Revelation 22:12
"Look, *I am* coming soon! My reward is with me, and I will give to each person according to what they have done."

Revelation 22:13
"*I am* the Alpha and the Omega, the First and the Last, the Beginning and the End."

Revelation 22:16
"I, Jesus, have sent my angel to give you this testimony for the churches. *I am* the Root and the Offspring of David, and the bright Morning Star."

Revelation 22:20

He who testifies to these things says, "Yes, *I am* coming soon." Amen. Come, LORD Jesus.

APPENDIX B

BIBLICAL GUIDELINES FOR HEALTHY RELATIONSHIPS

When we want to know how we are to treat others, we simply have to look through the New Testament. It is full of great insights for the way God expects us to interact.

"One Another" Passages

John 13:34
"A new command I give you: Love *one another.* As I have loved you, so you must love *one another.*"

John 13:35
"By this everyone will know that you are my disciples, if you love *one another.*"

Romans 12:10
Be devoted to *one another* in love. Honor *one another* above yourselves.

Romans 12:16
Live in harmony with *one another.* Do not be proud, but be willing to associate with people of low position. Do not be conceited.

Romans 13:8
Let no debt remain outstanding, except the continuing debt to love *one another,* for whoever loves others has fulfilled the law.

Romans 14:13
Therefore let us stop passing judgment on *one another.* Instead, make up your mind not to put any stumbling block or obstacle in the way of a brother or sister.

Romans 15:7
Accept *one another,* then, just as Christ accepted you, in order to bring praise to God.

Romans 15:14
I myself am convinced, my brothers and sisters, that you yourselves are full of goodness, filled with knowledge and competent to instruct *one another.*

Romans 16:16
Greet *one another* with a holy kiss. All the churches of Christ send greetings.

1 Corinthians 1:10
I appeal to you, brothers and sisters, in the name of our LORD Jesus Christ, that all of you agree with *one another* in what you say and that there be no divisions among you, but that you be perfectly united in mind and thought.

1 Corinthians 16:20
All the brothers and sisters here send you greetings. Greet *one another* with a holy kiss.

2 Corinthians 13:11
Finally, brothers and sisters, rejoice! Strive for full restoration, encourage *one another,* be of one mind, live in peace. And the God of love and peace will be with you.

2 Corinthians 13:12
Greet *one another* with a holy kiss.

Galatians 5:13
You, my brothers and sisters, were called to be free. But do not use your freedom to indulge the flesh; rather, serve *one another* humbly in love.

Ephesians 4:2
Be completely humble and gentle; be patient, bearing with *one another* in love.

Ephesians 4:32
Be kind and compassionate to *one another*, forgiving each other, just as in Christ God forgave you.

Ephesians 5:19
[Speak] to *one another* with psalms, hymns, and songs from the Spirit. Sing and make music from your heart to the LORD.

Ephesians 5:21
Submit to *one another* out of reverence for Christ.

Philippians 2:5
In your relationships with *one another*, have the same mindset as Christ Jesus.

Colossians 3:13
Bear with each other and forgive *one another* if any of you has a grievance against someone. Forgive as the LORD forgave you.

Colossians 3:16
Let the message of Christ dwell among you richly as you teach and admonish *one another* with all wisdom through psalms, hymns, and songs from the Spirit, singing to God with gratitude in your hearts.

1 Thessalonians 4:18
Therefore encourage *one another* with these words.

1 Thessalonians 5:11
Therefore encourage *one another* and build each other up, just as in fact you are doing.

2 Thessalonians 1:3
We ought always to thank God for you, brothers and sisters, and rightly so, because your faith is growing more and more, and the love all of you have for *one another* is increasing.

Hebrews 3:13
But encourage *one another* daily, as long as it is called "Today," so that none of you may be hardened by sin's deceitfulness.

Hebrews 10:24
And let us consider how we may spur *one another* on toward love and good deeds.

Hebrews 10:25
Not giving up meeting together, as some are in the habit of doing, but encouraging *one another*—and all the more as you see the Day approaching.

Hebrews 13:1
Keep on loving *one another* as brothers and sisters.

James 4:11
Brothers and sisters, do not slander *one another*. Anyone who speaks against a brother or sister or judges them speaks against the law and judges it. When you judge the law, you are not keeping it, but sitting in judgment on it.

James 5:9
Don't grumble against *one another*, brothers and sisters, or you will be judged. The Judge is standing at the door!

1 Peter 1:22
Now that you have purified yourselves by obeying the truth so that you have sincere love for each other, love *one another* deeply, from the heart.

1 Peter 3:8
Finally, all of you, be like-minded, be sympathetic, love *one another,* be compassionate and humble.

1 Peter 4:9
Offer hospitality to *one another* without grumbling.

1 Peter 5:5
In the same way, you who are younger, submit yourselves to your elders. All of you, clothe yourselves with humility toward *one another,* because, "God opposes the proud but shows favor to the humble."

1 Peter 5:14
Greet *one another* with a kiss of love. Peace to all of you who are in Christ.

1 John 1:7
But if we walk in the light, as he is in the light, we have fellowship with *one another,* and the blood of Jesus, his Son, purifies us from all sin.

1 John 3:11
For this is the message you heard from the beginning: We should love *one another.*

1 John 3:23
And this is his command: to believe in the name of his Son, Jesus Christ, and to love *one another* as he commanded us.

1 John 4:7
Dear friends, let us love *one another,* for love comes from God. Everyone who loves has been born of God and knows God.

1 John 4:11
Dear friends, since God so loved us, we also ought to love *one another.*

1 John 4:12
No one has ever seen God; but if we love *one another,* God lives in us and his love is made complete in us.

2 John 1:5
And now, dear lady, I am not writing you a new command but one we have had from the beginning. I ask that we love *one another.*

"Each Other" Passages

Romans 15:5
May the God who gives endurance and encouragement give you the same attitude of mind toward *each other* that Christ Jesus had.

1 Corinthians 12:25
So that there should be no division in the body, but that its parts should have equal concern for *each other.*

Galatians 5:26
Let us not become conceited, provoking and envying *each other.*

Colossians 3:9
Do not lie to *each other,* since you have taken off your old self with its practices.

1 Thessalonians 3:12
May the LORD make your love increase and overflow for *each other* and for everyone else, just as ours does for you.

1 Thessalonians 5:13
Hold them in the highest regard in love because of their work. Live in peace with *each other.*

1 Thessalonians 5:15
Make sure that nobody pays back wrong for wrong, but always strive to do what is good for *each other* and for everyone else.

James 5:16
Therefore confess your sins to *each other* and pray for *each other* so that you may be healed. The prayer of a righteous person is powerful and effective.

1 Peter 4:8
Above all, love *each other* deeply, because love covers over a multitude of sins.

"Others" Passages

1 Corinthians 10:24
No one should seek their own good, but the good of *others*.

Ephesians 4:29
Do not let any unwholesome talk come out of your mouths, but only what is helpful for building *others* up according to their needs, that it may benefit those who listen.

Philippians 2:3
Do nothing out of selfish ambition or vain conceit. Rather, in humility value *others* above yourselves.

Philippians 2:4
Not looking to your own interests but each of you to the interests of the *others*.

1 Peter 4:10
Each of you should use whatever gift you have received to serve *others*, as faithful stewards of God's grace in its various forms.

ABOUT THE AUTHOR

Kerry Clarensau is the Director of a national Christian women's organization with over 240,000 members. She is a credentialed minister, a mentor, and an international speaker. A prolific writer, she creates training materials and Internet resources for ministry to women and is the author of *Secrets: Transforming Your Life and Marriage* and *Love Revealed.*

Kerry and her husband, Mike, have two sons, Tyler and Blake; a daughter-in-law, Katie; and a granddaughter, Molly Jayne.

To learn more about Kerry and her ministry visit her online at www.KerryClarensau.com.

TO ORDER MORE COPIES

FOREWORD BY CAROL KENT

REDEEMED!

EMBRACING A
TRANSFORMED LIFE

KERRY CLARENSAU

TO ORDER MORE COPIES OF THIS BOOK VISIT
WWW.MYHEALTHYCHURCH.COM